IRON MAIDENS

IRON MAIDENS

The CELEBRATION of the MOST AWESOME FEMALE MUSCLE in the WORLD

KRISTIN KAYE

THUNDER'S MOUTH PRESS
NEW YORK

IRON MAIDENS

THE CELEBRATION OF THE MOST AWESOME FEMALE MUSCLE IN THE WORLD

Published by
Thunder's Mouth Press
An Imprint of Avalon Publishing Group Inc.
245 West 17th St., 11th Floor
New York, NY 10011

AVALON
publishing group incorporated

First printing September 2005

"Beefed-up Cheesecake Hopes to Make a Ripple" by John O'Mahony reprinted with permission from the *New York Post,* 1993, Copyright, NYP Holdings, Inc.

All photos © Bjorg Magnea

Library of Congress Cataloging-in-Publication Data is available.

ISBN 1-56025-704-0

9 8 7 6 5 4 3 2 1

Book design by Maria Elias
Printed in Canada
Distributed by Publishers Group West

To Jem and Siddha,
without whom words would have no meaning

Contents

Acknowledgments

A book is rarely a solitary effort. This book could not have been written without Colleene Colley and Dianné Aldrich, whose remarkable memories, keen observations, and zany humor helped piece this story together; those in the bodybuilding community who generously gave their time and insights in interviews: Robin Parker, Steve Wennerstrom, Sheila Bleck, Bill Dobbins, Dawn Whitham, Linda Wood-Hoyte, Lisa Bavington, Charles Peeples, Al Dauber, Bill Wick, Colette Guimond, Cheryl Harris, John Nafpliotis, Kenny Kassel, Leslie Heywood, Cynthia James, Annie Rivechio, and Mimi Jabalee; the early support of Jessica Morrell and the PDX women's writing crew; the steady eye of Michael McGregor; the all-around know-how of Jainee MacCarroll; and the masterful ushering of my agent, Stephanie Kip-Rostan. Thanks also to the many others who listened, discussed, read, and reread. Thank you for helping me bring this book to life.

Prologue:

Beefed-up Cheesecake Hopes to Make a Ripple

By John O'Mahony
New York Post Weekend Plus
Friday, November 5, 1993

V isualize the embrace—a love-hungry, passionate couple entwined in one another's arms.

But this is no ordinary couple. The woman can lift 240-pound men over her head and burst footballs—it takes 2,000 pounds of pressure—by squeezing them between her thighs.

The man? Well, through his mind are running visions of the black widow spider. He knows that one false move and those loving arms could break his neck. His muscular lady love is in total control.

How's that for a turn-on? No great shakes, say most men.

But Doughdee Marie, a vivacious, playful, 5-foot-2 blond bundle of muscle, cannot understand why any man could ever be repulsed or intimidated by women bodybuilders.

"Most men don't know that it's incredible to have a big strong woman like me hold them," she said. "To know that they have no control of the situation. To know that at any moment I cold break off any part of them. It may be scary, but believe me, it's sexy."

Doughdee, a Californian, is one of twenty women who take over the Roseland Ballroom at 7:30 tonight to stage their show, *The Celebration of the Most Awesome Female Muscle in the World*.

Organized by a New York bodybuilder—4-foot-10, 137-pound Laurie Fierstein—the show is a demonstration of her premise that a woman's body can—and should be—whatever a woman herself wants it to be. She hopes tonight to redefine the meaning of femininity when her bodybuilding friends strut the stage to perform dances, gymnastics, and feats of strength.

"I want to show the bodybuilding community and the world at large that muscle and womanhood are not diametrically opposed," she said. "Why should the stereotype for women be those who are delicate and weak? Why shouldn't women be strong and powerful?"

Adds Millie Carter, 160 pounds with seven major titles to show for her eight years of pumping iron: "I've seen lots of skimpy, skinny girls and there's nothing at all feminine about them."

All the women, however, are aware that there is

entrenched opposition to their idea of beauty—the bulging biceps, seemingly bosomless chests, and gaunt cheeks that characterize women who seek to reinvent themselves in gyms.

Even among themselves there is disagreement.

Doughdee, who came to weightlifting for rehabilitation from injuries while a professional ice skater—and who considers herself an entertainer rather than a bodybuilder—believes that some women have pushed their physiques too far.

"Women need some fat to be beautiful. It's when they slim down below 4 percent fat—and that's dangerous healthwise—and their breasts disappear that people are inclined to say, 'That's disgusting, she looks like a man,'" she said.

But Brooklyn sculptor Robin Parker, who says she has changed her medium from bronze to muscle, argues that the American male is just plain fixated on breasts.

She added—a reply to men who can't see beyond chests—"A well-built arm can be absolutely stunning looking. And don't tell me bodybuilders don't have good butts."

Fierstein, too, dismisses the critics. She is adamant that there should be no constraints as far as taking bodies to their absolute limits.

"There's no such thing as too far. Women should take their bodies in hand and go as far as they want for muscle and leanness," she said. "Remember, bodybuilding is a form of empowerment for a woman and as such a metaphor for the other aspects of her life."

It is this sense of taking control that drives Fierstein and the other women who share her view.

"The first time I lifted up a weight, I found it thrilling," she said. "Immediately, there was a sense of achievement in being able to lift an immovable object. Also, you see you can change things and before long there's concrete proof, because the results of your efforts are on your body."

Now that the constraints of the female physique have been challenged and overcome, the next step for Fierstein and her friends is to confront the world's perception—especially the ingrained male perception—of the results.

"When men are repulsed by female muscle, their view does not come from an intrinsic aesthetic," Fierstein said. "What's needed is more exposure—like at this show. I believe that men, given some re-education, can come to accept all forms of the female body, of which this is one. And I know that someday they will even come to like it."

1

Meet Laurie Fierstein

When Laurie Fierstein spoke, her words were steady and deliberate, like a roller coaster cranking its way up. Her words had a course, a direction. "I am one of the most muscular women in the world," she said when we first met. She qualified this statement with the fact that she was forty-three years old and then giggled with glee. She had a staccato laugh whose melody rose and then fell in turns, a goofy exhale on her joyride flying right into the face of what the world expected.

Her laugh said "Wheeee! Look at me." You couldn't help but notice.

At 4 feet 10 inches, she stood almost as wide as she was tall, the circumference of her neck equaling that of my thigh. The bulk of her arms and back was so massive it kept her arms from lying flat against her sides, forcing them to swing in wide arcs. She could spread the muscles in her back the way a peacock fans its tail. When she did this and dug her fists into her hips, the position known within the bodybuilding world as a lat spread, there was no space left between the sides of her body and the crook of her mammoth arm. Her thighs measured in at approximately 26 inches (picture a soccer ball) and her calves bulged to 17 (think big cantaloupe). Her back narrowed like a V to a dense waist that produced mounds that were small boulder-like glutes. The girth of Laurie's thighs forced her to walk with a slight waddle. At a competition weight of 130 pounds and an off-season weight of 162 pounds, either way you could say she was densely packed.

One of the first things she told me was, "I've always challenged the status quo." It started with things like frogstands and hula-hoops. She once held a frogstand—that's when you lean forward on your hands, wedge your knees onto your elbows, then lift your feet off the ground, and balance—for two hours, and another time she hula-hooped for twenty-three hours straight. Later she moved on to more serious issues like overpriced meat. In 1973 Laurie led a class-action lawsuit against the beef industry. Because of her efforts, six of the country's largest beef companies found themselves appearing before a judge in a Manhattan federal district court. The case hit the front page of national papers such as the *New York Times* and the *Boston Globe*. From the age of fourteen, whether it was a march for the homeless or hungry children, you could bet that Laurie either organized it or was in the crowd.

One could argue that her provocative disposition is genetic. Laurie's mother, Hannah Tompkins, is an artist and a national authority on Shakespeare. Her father, Irving Fierstein, is also an artist, renowned for his depictions of social injustice. His painting of the jailhouse beating of Fanny Lou Hamer hangs in the Martin Luther King Jr. Memorial in Atlanta, Georgia; his most famous piece, *Free South Africa*, depicts two black hands breaking chains over a map of Africa. He is also a chess enthusiast and a marathoner who just so happened to complete a full marathon at the agile age of seventy-four.

Laurie got to be one of the world's most muscular

women more or less by accident. In her early thirties she began lifting weights to recover from an injury and loved it immediately: the feeling of pitting herself against the weight, pushing her body, watching it transform. The idea of transformation was even more addicting than the exercise—her body against a stack of weights that should be immovable but, as a result of her will, wasn't. Such as a 1,200-pound leg press, a 185-pound behind-the-neck seated shoulder press, 225-pound weighted chin-ups, and 415-pound squats.

What started as rehab turned into serious training. A typical bodybuilder's day starts at around 5 A.M. on the StairMaster (before eating anything) and doing cardio for 45 minutes to kick-start the metabolism so the body will more quickly burn up the breakfast to come. Then it's time for work. Laurie, like many bodybuilders, became a personal trainer. It makes it easier to fit in two workouts a day, usually an hour in the morning and an hour in the afternoon, each day focusing on a different area of the body: either the back, arms, abs, or legs. The goal is to target a specific muscle and then lift a certain amount of weight eight to twelve times, as much as it takes for the muscle to become exhausted. Then you rest, add more weight, and repeat the set three to four times, each time pushing the muscle to failure. Failure is essential because it forces the muscle to adapt and get stronger. Basically, failure and exhaustion are how you grow muscles. This is repeated six days a week.

In 1990, a fellow bodybuilder talked Laurie into competing with him in a couple's posing competition. She was not entirely thrilled about walking around in heels and a bikini, but decided to give it a try. She dropped twenty-five pounds for the competition. Her partner dropped out, but she resolved to compete alone and came in second. Even more than winning, Laurie discovered she loved being seen. She was proud of what she had done with her body and wanted to show herself off. After her victory, she wanted to get even bigger and then willed her new body into existence.

Everything in life Laurie took on was huge in nature and she did it with an odd combination of steady perseverance and nonchalance, paying little attention to the bigness of the task. Whether it was twenty-three hours of hula-hooping, challenging the beef industry, or undertaking the complete transformation of her body, when Laurie decided she wanted to do something, it would be done. She was greatly amused watching the world react to her actions, like the time when two New York City cops pulled her aside in the subway to check out the size of her biceps. "What, is it a crime?" she recounted, her laugh climbing its way up.

When I met her in 1993, Laurie was taking on no less than the entire world of bodybuilding, which, when judging women's bodies in competition included femininity in its list of evaluative criteria (a standard that had no equivalent in the evaluation of men). Since the advent of female bodybuilding in the early 1980s, getting "big" was not considered feminine, so the International Federation of BodyBuilders, the governing body of the competitive bodybuilding world, told the judges that women could get big, but not to the extreme. No one knew exactly what that meant, especially because sometimes the IFBB made femininity an official criterion and other times, in response to public reaction, made it unofficial but still urged the judges to take it into consideration. The end result was that in the early 1990s, women who were exploding with muscle, pushing the limits of what the female body had ever been known to do, were losing to smaller, softer women. This infuriated Laurie. "Since when do we tell athletes to be good but not *too* good at what they do? And what does having muscles have to do with femininity?" She decided to take action. "I'm throwing down the gauntlet to the world that imposes limitations on me," she said. And so she did. That was how she decided to create *The Celebration of the Most Awesome Female Muscle in the World*.

It was also how her path crossed mine—a fateful moment when I believed I had been no less than divinely delivered to my destiny. This is how it happened.

2

The Celebration: Act I, Scene 1

I t all began so perfectly.

It was September 1993. A self-proclaimed performance artist recently graduated from drama school just outside of New York, I had rented a room in a farmhouse on an eighty-acre apple orchard fifty miles north of Manhattan, where I planned to create art that was important. (Truth is, I was too intimidated by the big city to actually live there.) Before any masterpiece could be birthed, however, I had one small task to contend with.

Just loosed from parental purse strings, I had to find a job to make money to pay rent.

I was scouring the *Village Voice* classifieds for work when I came upon the following ad: "Administrative assistant wanted for exciting women's project." In college, I had discovered the word "womyn" with a *y* and had experimented with growing my body hair. You could say I had feminist tendencies, though the word "feminist" felt like a relic from a bygone era of rallies and hippie beads; it seemed more suited to providing freedom from what I considered the plight of my girlhood Girl Scout leader, who baked incessantly, barely moved her mouth when she sang the Girl Scout Honor Song, and wore overly starched dresses that made me itch when I just looked at them. The point is I didn't even bother to circle the ad. I called right away, thinking, "This is excellent. Ten bucks an hour for a cool cause."

Laurie's voice charged across the phone line and into my ear. She wouldn't tell me much except that she needed help with a theatrical revue celebrating twenty-five of the world's strongest and most muscular women scheduled to take place at New York City's famous Roseland Ballroom. The caveat—there was a good chance the position was already filled.

I quickly got over the loss of the job and focused on the situation at hand. It was better than perfect. It was the ultimate—theater about women's strength on Broadway. Well, half a block away on Fifty-second Street, surely Roseland was still considered Broadway. Whatever, it was close enough for me. I knew I had seconds to get my foot in the door and quickly ran through my theatrical credentials— playwright, director, performance artist, stage manager, all-around theater buff willing to work for, ahem, very little money for the right project. I didn't need to tell her that was all for school performances, did I? I offered my services should she find herself in need of a little help with the dramatic side of the project. I promised to send a video of my work and she promised to keep me in mind.

One week later, there was a message on my answering machine. Laurie was interested in talking to me about being the playwright and director of *The Celebration*. I gasped. Here it was. My Big Break calling me up. I wrote down her number and immediately returned the call. A man answered.

"'Ullo." His accent was the thickest I'd ever heard in New York.

"Hi, I'm looking for Laurie Fierstein." I thought I would choke.

"Who?"

"Um, Laurie. Laurie Fierstein."

"Nevah heard of huh. Ya got the wrawng numbah."

Panic. It couldn't be wrong. I had just written it down. "Are you sure?"

"Dunno who yawr tawlkin' ahbowt."

"Well she just called and gave me this number. She has to be there." I was not accepting this.

"I dunno whadda say. Wait. Hold on. Wait, wait, wait. I think I might know huh. Yeah, I see huh. Hold on." He muffled the phone, but I could hear him calling. "Lawrie, yo, Lawr. Phone cawl." The phone clanked against a hard surface. After a minute, she picked it up.

"Hello?" There she was! "Who's this?" She sounded startled.

"Hi, Laurie, this is me, Kristin. I'm just returning your call. I got your message and I'd love to be the playwright and director."

"How'd you get this phone number?" She sounded suspicious.

"Well, you left it on the answering machine." This was not the response I was expecting.

"I couldn't have."

"What do you mean? I just wrote it down from your message."

"Kristin, this is the pay phone in the gym I work out in. I don't even know this phone number. I wouldn't know this number if you shook me upside down to get it."

"What?" Everything was now odd.

"I left you my home number." She proceeded to tell me the number she had left. I compared it to what I had written down and realized I had switched two of the digits. The number I dialed happened to be the pay phone at her gym in Manhattan and she happened to be working out. A moment of silence passed as we tried to grasp the significance of what had just happened.

After numerous blurts of "Oh my God, I can't believe this," she continued with conviction. "Well, this is definitely a sign. So, do you want the job? I mean it's clear to me, it's meant to be."

All I could do was jump up and down and say, "Yes, yes, yes!"

Broadway. I was going to be on Broadway. Or Off-Broadway. I didn't even know which, but it didn't matter. This was it. My Big Break. This was going to be one of those moments that you look back on and see how your whole world changed—a moment when you gleefully accept that, as much as you think you control the events of your life, there just might be a greater plan.

At least that's what I thought at the time.

Truth is, I had no idea about the world I was about to step into. Nor, at the age of twenty-three, did it dawn on me that it might be a good idea to find out. I was wont to dive head-first into life, knowing little except the rush of vertigo I felt free-falling into situations that happened to come my way. Had I been prepared, known even a little about what lay ahead—say, that normally sane interactions can turn otherwise when testosterone has been injected by one of the parties—everything might have turned out differently or maybe I wouldn't have taken the job at all. But, having serendipitously reached Laurie on the pay phone in the gym when it just so happened she was there working out gave me the distinct impression that fate was whispering to me, "This one's for you, kid. Dive, girl, dive!"

3

Athletics Make Women
Masculine (or So They Say)

——————

When women like Laurie started going to gyms in the late 1970s, they were often called things like "cunt" and "butch" and "lesbo" or they were simply told to go away. The gym in those days was more like a beefy men's club—to step inside was to enter hostile territory. Whether the women were doing a little injury rehab or actually building muscle, it didn't matter. They were blatantly ignored, excluded from the chummy banter that was tossed about between male lifters. That is, until they got fed up and did something rash, like lift more weight than the men did. That usually broke the spell.

Women lifting weights was confounding. What people wanted to know was, "Why do you want muscles? Why do you want to look like a man?" Mind you, by today's standards, originally set by titans such as Arnold Schwarzenegger, the "muscular" bodies of the late seventies and early eighties looked more like Jane Fonda when she started doing her exercise thing: nicely trim with long, lean muscle that accentuated female curves. Bulk was not yet in vogue. But the mere gesture of placing a female hand on a barbell and lifting it in repetition seemed to suggest inevitable masculinity.

This concern was nothing new, however. Doctors way back at the turn of the twentieth century were worried that sport of any kind might make women more masculine. Dr. Dudley Allen Sargent, a Harvard University professor and founder of the Sargent School of Physical Training, which became the Sargent College of Health and Rehabilitation Sciences at Boston University five years after his death in 1924, studied and wrote extensively on the effects of athletics on both men and women. He had a huge impact on the field of physical and outdoor education. In 1912, Sargent published a paper entitled "Are Athletics Making Girls Masculine? A Practical Answer to a Question Every Girl Asks." In the paper he lamented, "Every journalistic wind that blows either moans or shrieks, according to its source, of feminine activities, and we are forced to listen whether we will or not. Much of the reading matter put forth in certain somewhat sensational papers so utterly disregards truth and reason that we are in danger of half believing that womankind has already become a distorted Amazon creation, to be talked about and wondered at, but no longer to be loved and admired."

Sargent had some, shall we say, interesting ideas. He began his paper by pointing out that biologists of his day believed humans are dual in nature: men and women are a combination of both sexes. Secondary sexual characteristics are lying in wait most likely to make an appearance later in life or under the influence of certain habits or habitats. For centuries, men and women led more or less the same lifestyle and were more alike. It has only been since humans have become highly civilized, he explained, that there has been such divergence between the sexes.

Sargent went on to describe a particularly curious phenomenon. Due to a variable he called the "law of chance" when we are born we inherit anywhere from one-tenth to nine-tenths of our characteristics from either our mother's side or our father's side. In other words, a boy can be eight-tenths his mother and two-tenths his father and will probably be lousy at sports. Likewise, a girl can be nine-tenths her father and one-tenth her mother and be able to kick a mean penalty shot. According to Sargent, 25 percent of men and women inherit equally from both parents.

Sargent suggested that it is important for a girl to consider her level of masculinity, either inherited or acquired, when choosing her sport. For example, lawn tennis, fencing, swimming, hurdling, and bowling are all sports more natural to women because they tend to broaden the hips, which is a feminine characteristic. A girl can't expect to do very well at things like rowing and handling heavy weights without broadening her waist and shoulders, which is not feminine. Sports like boxing, baseball, wrestling, and water polo will make women masculine in an objectionable sense, mainly because they are so strenuous and have the potential for violent encounters. These factors are important to consider for men as well who have predominantly feminine characteristics.

Sargent was all for girls playing sports, but he proposed that men's athletics be modified for girls— in light of "the peculiar constitution of her nervous system and the great emotional disturbances to which she is subjected" and to lessen the possibility of girls becoming more masculine. For example, he thought that reducing the playing time and lengthening rest periods, lowering the height of hurdles and shortening distances, and increasing the number of players on teams would help prevent exhaustion, a state that incurs a "fearful cost to themselves and eventually their children." According to Sargent, slow, careful preparation and intelligent supervision would ensure the protection of femininity.

Despite these concerns, girls and women have been setting athletic records for centuries: In 1857, Julia Archibald Holmes—wearing a dress, bloomers, moccasins, and a hat—was the first woman to reach the summit of Colorado's Pikes Peak (14,110 feet); the U.S. Open crowned the first women's singles champion, Lottie Dodd, in 1887; nineteen women competed in the Olympics in 1900 in tennis, golf, and croquet; in 1901, Annie Taylor, a woman who couldn't swim, was the first person to go over Niagara Falls in a custom-built barrel and live (she declared, "Nobody ever ought to do that again"); in Iowa in 1904, sixteen-year old Amanda Clement became the first female umpire to officiate at a men's baseball game for pay.

Skipping through the decades, piles of records have been set by women the likes of pilot Amelia Earhart, Olympic athletes such as the golfer Babe Didrikson and the track star Wilma Rudolph, and the tennis pro Billie Jean King, who, among scores of victories, won the now-famous "battle-of-the-sexes" tennis match in 1973 against Bobby Riggs. Riggs had challenged her to a game, claiming that she, being a woman, was no match for his manhood, despite the fact that he was twenty-five years her senior. Before 50 million television viewers, she beat him in three straight sets.

This victory—riding on the wave of 1960s feminism and coupled with Title IX of the Education Amendments of 1972, legislation requiring equal rights for males and females in education and sports—marked the beginnings of an explosion in athleticism for women. Before the act was passed, 31,000 high school girls were playing inter-scholastic sports. Today, the number is well above 3 million.

Coincidentally, female athletic performance has also experienced a dramatic spike, while male performance is reaching natural limits. In a 2003 article in the *New York*

Times, "A Strength Not Yet Tested, Not Yet Known," a *Times* science writer, Gina Kolata, explores this phenomenon. She quotes Dr. Howard Wainer, a research scientist at the Board of Medical Examiners in Philadelphia, who explains, "Men are making improvements by the millimeter and women are making improvements by the yard." The difference has to do with athletic training. Women are not as strong as men physiologically, but, according to Catherine Jackson, head of the kinesiology department at California State University at Fresno, "it is amazing to see how much better women can get with athletic training. And they only began to train seriously in the last twenty years." The effects of training account for the leaps of progress that female athletes are experiencing. Experts predict that the years to come will see continued improvement.

I didn't know any of this when I was a kid in the 1970s. A Title IX baby, I was oblivious to the fact that I had stepped into the continuum at a point in time when it was natural for a girl not to think twice before playing whatever sport she wanted. Had I been born even ten years earlier I might have been able to play soccer, but there probably wouldn't have been uniforms or organized leagues or a school bus to take me to the game. As far as I was concerned, playing sports was as natural as using baby oil when I lay out in the sun. It was just what you did. Fall and spring were soccer season, winter was basketball, and summer was swimming. (Of course, as a tall girl, I still slouched into one hip to reduce my height by whatever amount possible because I knew that girls should be shorter than boys. But that was different.)

Women's bodybuilding followed a similar natural progression. Women kept getting bigger and better at cultivating their physiques. If the International Federation of BodyBuilders had measured the biceps of female competitors from the 1970s to today, they probably would have documented an increase of about an inch a decade. Around 1990, when I met Laurie, the average bicep might have measured in at close to 17 inches, up from 15 in the late 1970s. One thing, however, remained constant—in competitions, judges would consider femininity along with the traditional evaluative criteria: muscular symmetry, proportion, definition, separation, and muscularity. Considering that the women bulked their trunk and limbs as thick as trees and dieted themselves down to close to zero percent body fat (nearly guaranteeing the disappearance of their breasts) just how, exactly, she could score high on the "femininity" factor was the question on every competitor's lips.

4

The Celebration: Act I, Scene 2

I am sometimes prone to fantasy.

Before I went to Manhattan to meet Laurie for the first time, New York City worried me. When I visited from fifty miles north, where I had lived since I was twelve, I was scared of getting lost. Not lost in the physical sense, because New York has a pretty straightforward north–south, east–west grid, but lost in the way white water snatches a leaf from shore and tumbles it in its torrents until the leaf disappears completely. I worried that the city would swallow me whole, swirling and twirling me into oblivion.

I limited my visits to just a few hours. I never strayed from the 6 subway line, which whisked me directly from Grand Central downtown to Astor Place, where I would walk one block west to Broadway. From there, I went directly south a few blocks to the Canal Jeans Clothing Company, then west a few blocks to the Olive Tree restaurant on MacDougal (where they had great hot borscht and you could draw on the tables with chalk), and then back to the 6 subway line at Astor Place. I'm not exactly sure what I thought would happen if I stepped onto another street or entered a different neighborhood, but I was convinced it couldn't be good.

Yet for all my worry, there were equal parts awe. Before my visits, I would spend a day preparing, trying to concoct an outfit that would exude urban chic. I felt like an imposter trying to be like the exotic beings in Greenwich Village. Whatever their variety, they were effortlessly cool and always busy with something that seemed to matter. Life *happened* there, and I longed for it to happen to me. And then the phone call happened. And changed everything.

On that day in September, when I went to meet Laurie, instead of making my usual beeline through

Grand Central from my train to the 6 subway, suspiciously eyeing everyone around me, squeezing my bag tightly to my ribs under one arm, I walked right out the front entrance onto Forty-second Street. I took Manhattan ten blocks at a time down the West Side, walking above the earth. Three feet, in fact, was my cruising altitude, my graceful glide from Midtown to West Twenty-second Street in Chelsea.

The shrieking throng of lunchtime workers imposed not even the slightest shove, and a single ray of the golden sun warmed the top of my head against the coming chill of fall. The city's timeless stars were everywhere. There were Frank Sinatra and Gene Kelly rehearsing *On the Town*, dressed in pressed white navy uniforms, winking at me as they filed into a cab; Andy Warhol waved down from his scaffolding, strung precariously above the seething knot of Times Square, where he was industriously painting my face in repetition. Down Broadway, the dancers from *Cats* slunk their lithe bodies before me to part the Sea of Manhattan so I wouldn't be late for my first day of work. Me, the girl from fifty miles north of Manhattan. But they all knew who I was. I was the Chosen One. I was the playwright and director of *The Celebration of the Most Awesome Female Muscle in the World*.

So when Laurie opened the door to greet me, I was only partly flummoxed to shake hands with five feet of pure muscle. Standing together in the glow of the foyer lamp, me so much taller than her, I could look down at the part in her hair as I tried to return the grip of her handshake, smiling through our greeting, working to maintain my composure. Having attended art school, I'd been exposed to my fair share of arty types and extreme freaks, so I wasn't completely green. But, truth is, to look at her was to be in shock.

The dialogue inside my head started with "Wow!" and then went to "Oh my," and then back to "Wow!" I was strangely surprised to hear a sparky yet honey-smooth "Hello" emit from that body—if a superhero action figure started speaking, you'd look for the ventriloquist. But when she spoke, she was just another person, and I ceased to think about her body. I simply related to her directly. Then, she turned to take me into her apartment, and there was her body again, dressed in knee-length, black athletic tights, thick, gym socks, sneakers, and a T-shirt with rolled up sleeves. Her skin, tanned and cured, was stretched taut over pectoral muscles, deltoids, biceps, and triceps that were cities thriving just beneath the surface: hard, tough, and unyielding, asserting themselves on the world. But that's not right, not cities. Nations. No, not nations. Whole continents. Each muscle group was a landmass jutting up and out, demanding evolution.

The apartment was a first-floor studio, but in New York terms that means a shoebox with a bathroom and, if you're lucky, a closet for a kitchen. New Yorkers are masters of "cross-purpose" living. The spaces are so small they're forced to use one room for many functions. Laurie was one of the lucky ones, with a studio of approximately five hundred square feet separated into two rooms by an arched walkway that probably prompted the landlord to advertise it as a one-bedroom, even though there was no door to the second room. By day her apartment was a full-fledged production office. In one half of the apartment, let's call it the living room–dining room area, a round wooden table piled high with papers and stuffed manila folders monopolized the center of the space, leaving little room to pass. A computer and telephone obscured a small desk that was crammed into a corner. The walls were covered with large month-at-a-glance erasable calendars, typed schedules, and to-do lists, and at least two-dozen 8-by-10-inch glossies of female bodybuilders she was considering for the show. In the next "room," a floral comforter–covered bed doubled as a couch where one could sit to chat with people sitting in the living–dining room area or to watch TV. The set sat precariously on a small stand in the far corner. Light squeaked in from the barred window behind the TV. A bureau narrowed the short hallway leading to the bathroom and kitchen closets. By night, Laurie probably just pushed the stuff aside to make way for dinner and sleeping. I would learn that's the way it is in New York; if you want something, it's up to you to make it happen no matter what gets in the way.

"Have a seat. I'll be just a second." Manicured fingernails extending from her mountainous arm pointed me to a chair that was occupied by a cat. "That's Mr. Kitty. Just shove him off." Mr. Kitty, however, was not shove-off-able. His sheer mass convinced me that he was fed protein shakes in his kitty bowl. He wasn't having any part of my moving him. There wasn't another free chair in the place, and I was not going to stand, so I squeezed into the space left on the chair, intending to intimidate him off by virtue of being at least twenty times his size.

"You'll have to forgive me." She returned from the kitchen munching a hunk of skinless chicken breast wrapped in tin foil. "It's feeding time." She giggled a surprisingly girlish giggle. "So, you must be wanting to know what you've gotten yourself into."

I did, but the buzz from the cosmic occurrence still lingered and had a similar effect as laughing gas. I was giddy and happy and not as concerned as I should have been about details.

Laurie was a sparkplug perched on the edge of a chair, unfolding her vision. "I am an intellectual physique artist," she began. Her musculature prohibited her from lounging lazily, and I'd swear she had puffed up her chest as if she were holding her breath, except that she was breathing normally. Shoulder-length brown, gently wavy hair curled around a face that was round like a full moon with shining dark eyes and a wide mouth that willingly produced an even wider grin. She talked about ancient matriarchal Amazon cultures and roaming robust Dianas and the absurdity of limiting anyone who wants to better themselves the way some people talk about the weather. So very la-dee-da. Yet, you could feel her conviction like bedrock and almost hear an anthem playing in the background. Her particular kind of charisma made it all sound so simple and so obvious that it was easy to be folded into her vision and I found myself arriving at the same conclusions she did. "But of course! A Broadway extravaganza is the perfect way to win the war over femininity in competitive bodybuilding." Everything was eminently achievable. And then she broke the spell with her laugh that was silly and infectious and manic and softened her.

"What I'm basically trying to do here is remove the constraints that have been applied to the female, body-builders and nonathletes alike. How women are viewed in the competitive bodybuilding world is a reflection of the way we view women in every facet of society: they're only allowed to go so far," she explained.

The smooth flow of her thoughts made it sound as if she'd said the words many times before, if only to herself, as if by repeating them the ideas would grow as large and solid as her body.

"The way it shows up in bodybuilding is by telling them they can be muscular, but only up to a point. What I am saying is that there is no point. There are no limits. We have to allow each woman to be whatever and who-ever she wants to be. She should never have to ask anyone, not judges, not anyone, how she should look. That's only for her to decide."

As she spoke, I didn't want to gawk, but I couldn't help staring at her shoulders and arms. My eyes strug-gled to meet hers, but I found myself following the con-tour of her rounded shoulders, the bulging tributaries of her veins, wondering if she ever felt small inside herself, if she ever felt she had to yell to make her voice louder than her body.

"It's been such a sorry state of affairs for women that we've been told how to look," she continued. "*The Celebration* will break down those barriers. And it's your job to help these women transmit the magic of their personas to the audience."

And that wasn't all. Laurie wanted to celebrate strength in the intellectual realm as well. She wanted me to adapt literature from writers like Alice Walker and Edna St. Vincent Millay and write original material for the emcee segments between performers. It was to be a theatrical extravaganza. Eighteen of the world's strongest and most muscular women were already on board, including power lifters and Olympic athletes. She was working on signing up another ten. She boasted support from Hollywood and interest from publications the likes of *Ms.* magazine and the *New Yorker*. It was already getting big. It was also September and *The Celebration* was scheduled for the first week in November. The women would not be in New York until two days before the performance, so I would have to plan and direct the entire show over the phone.

By now, a private panic had set in, and I decided it

might be a good idea to take notes. Over the course of our meeting, Mr. Kitty curled up in my lap, giving me more room on the chair. His purr rattled into the bones of my thighs as I balanced my note pad on the chair's arm, scribbling to keep up with Laurie's plans.

"It's amazing! These women can finally reach for the stars. The combination of physical strength, the theatrical layer, and the literature—well," she paused for a moment, her dark eyes flashing, transfixed by the vision in her head, "it's unprecedented." Then the laugh started cranking its way up. "It's nuts! It's just crazy. I can't believe this is happening."

I couldn't either. I had no idea how I was going to pull it off, but I was a sucker for big ideas, and it felt like Laurie's magic carpet had specifically stopped to take me along for the ride. Listening to her, I believed I was sitting in the middle of a great historical moment: that I had been chosen for this position to represent a new female voice, a voice that took the torch of feminism and carried it for a new generation. What that voice would say I had no idea about either, but I figured I'd come up with something.

I pictured myself on the cover of *Ms.* magazine with the headline "The New Female Voice" printed in large, bold, white letters. Gloria Steinem smiled down on me while I sat squarely facing the camera with a confidant half-smile.

At that point, swept up in the aura of her vision, I gripped Laurie's hand, smiled bravely, and said, "I don't believe in accidents. I know that I am meant to work on this show." And I honestly said, "I understand," when she explained there would be only a token amount of money to pay me. "I wouldn't be doing this for the money anyway," I said.

And so I glided back to Grand Central terminal. On the way, I helped Fay Wray. It was the least I could do.

5

A Sport Can Face Extinction, Too, Part I

I f you look up the word "extinction" in the third edition of the American Heritage College Dictionary, it will give the following definition: "*n.* The process or fact of disappearing completely from use; the decreasing or dying out of a behavioral response created by conditioning because of lack of reinforcement." If you consider the second definition, then women's bodybuilding has been facing extinction ever since it began. Some blame the slow demise on the tension between women's burgeoning muscles and the attempts by the International Federation of Body-Builders to limit that growth to a reasonable, "feminine" size. That camp wants to know, how can the sport prosper if women are effectively asked to atrophy, asked to stop short of achieving their full potential in the name of femininity? Others blame the female bodybuilders themselves, saying they are victims of their own success. If only they hadn't gotten so damn good at what they do, if only they hadn't gotten so big, the general public wouldn't be so uncomfortable with female muscle and the sport of bodybuilding could enjoy more acceptance.

But it isn't just the IFBB and the general public who seem uncomfortable with mountainous muscle on a female frame. Since the mid-1990s, sponsorship dollars, prize money, and press coverage for female competitors have dramatically decreased. Taken together, these obstacles are enough to convince fans of the sport that the industry is trying to snuff out female muscle altogether.

But determining whether or not female bodybuilding is actually facing extinction is tricky. Steve Wennerstrom, the official IFBB women's historian and the editor of *Women's Physique World*, cites data that show that the number of female competitors grew rapidly in the 1980s, decreased in the 1990s, but has been on the rise again since 2000. Bill Dobbins is an industry journalist and photographer who has published a number of coffee-table books on the subject and runs an extensive website featuring artistic photographic interpretations of female muscle and articles that chronicle the decades-long conundrum over judging the muscular female physique. He has a more philosophical take on the matter. According to Dobbins, female bodybuilding is doing just fine. All these barriers to success aren't really barriers at all; they're just natural reactions to the revolution that has been incited by bodacious brawn. The world will catch up in time. Until it does, factions on both sides of the femininity debate argue passionately for what they believe is best for the survival of the sport.

Documentary filmmakers Charles Gaines and George Butler captured the early stage of the dilemma in their 1983 film *Pumping Iron II: The Women*, a follow-up to *Pumping Iron*, the movie that launched Arnold Schwarzenegger on his rise to mega-stardom. *Pumping Iron II* followed five female bodybuilders as they prepared for and competed in the Caesars Palace World Cup Championship. Four of the women—Rachel McLish, Lori Bowen, Lydia Cheng, and Carla Dunlap—had lithe, lioness-like bodies.

And then there was the world's strongest female powerlifter, Australia's Bev Francis (affectionately known within the bodybuilding world as Bev), whose dream was to be as big as big could be. "I always admired strength in anything," she said in the film, "whether it was human or animal or the weather. I loved thunderstorms, anything that is big and strong and powerful, and I wanted to be powerful myself." She decided to leave lifting alone for a while and try bodybuilding on for size. She actually built muscles, the kind you see on football players, bulging, rippling muscles that exploded from her frame. No one had seen anything like Bev before. Filmmakers Gaines and Butler got Bev to enter the contest just to find out what would happen if a woman competed who actually pushed the limits of the female physique.

It caused problems for the judges. They wanted to know: What were they judging, an overall aesthetic that maintained femininity or the most built body? Where would they draw the line? Why was there a line being drawn at all? How could they tell an athlete that there was a point beyond which she could not go? Ben Weider, the founder and president of the IFBB, gathered the judges together to clarify the matter, to articulate once and for all how women bodybuilders should be judged. This is what he said: "This is the official IFBB analysis of the meaning of [femininity]. What we're looking for is something that's right down the middle, a woman who has a certain amount of aesthetic femininity, but yet has that muscle tone to show that she's an athlete. We are here to protect the majority and protect our sport. If you have the majority of the girls that absolutely say, 'Hey, let's go for these big, grotesque muscles, let's go for the ultimate,' so be it. But we are following what the majority wants. I just want to say that women are women and men are men and there's a difference and thank God for that difference. That's all I have to say."

When talking with the female competitors, describing to them how they would be assessed, an IFBB judge said, "The very first sentence in the women's rule book covers it. Judges must remember that they are judging a women's contest and the competitors must still look like women." A competitor countered, "But we all have our definitions of what looks like femininity." The judge ended the conversation by saying, "Well, if the women start going to extremes and looking like men, that's not what we are looking for in this contest. It's the results of this competition that will act as a guide and the judges are being briefed so they don't go to the extremes. It's the winners that will set what you might call the standards of femininity."

Like other fans of the sport, Bill Dobbins has been questioning the "standards of femininity" since he began covering women's bodybuilding in the early days for *Muscle and Fitness* magazine. Dobbins has used his position as one of the industry's leading journalists to challenge the IFBB and, for that matter, the world's assumptions about what a woman's body should look like. "People like myself and Wennerstrom have been pulling our hair out for twenty-something years fighting for the recognition and rights of female competitors; that what they are trying to achieve be considered as worthwhile as what the men have been trying to achieve."

Over the years, on three occasions the IFBB has invited Dobbins to write or update the rules for competition—only for the Federation re-write them when they felt they needed to re-address the femininity question. Dobbins used the following line of reasoning to establish equality when judging men and women: "You should be able to make the same statement logically for men as for women. For example, if you say that women shouldn't get so big and bulky that they lose their symmetry and proportion, can you say that about the men? Yes you can. Can you say that men shouldn't diet so hard that they look depleted onstage and look stringy and lose their shape? Can you say that about women? Yes you can. When women get too muscular and lose their femininity, what can you say that is comparable about men? You can't."

Bodybuilding's subjective judging system hasn't helped resolve the debate. It is easy to determine the winner of a track event. An objective fact—the fastest time—determines the winner. But bodybuilding, like ice skating or gymnastics, relies on judges' subjective opinions. Even in ice skating and gymnastics there are defined levels of technical difficulty, specific measures that help determine the best athlete—for example, in ice skating, a triple jump rather than a double. Not so in bodybuilding. Judges assess muscle shape, proportion, symmetry, separation, and muscularity—and, when it comes to the women, femininity. Judges are expected to have a trained eye that knows what a balanced, symmetrical physique looks like. Although there is no objective depiction of this desired state, typically it should include a small waist, a V-shape from the waist to shoulders, small joints, and muscles that are built in proportion to the competitor's frame.

Here's how a competition works. There are four rounds: two prejudging rounds and two finals rounds.

Prejudging takes place early in the day. In round 1, competitors line up onstage standing at ease. In unison they make four quarter turns to display each side of their physique. Three to five competitors may be called out of the line-up to stand front and center where the judges can better compare them. This is the crux of judging, comparing bodies to determine who has the best physique on that particular day. In round 2, competitors perform compulsory poses individually. When everyone has posed, the group is lined up again and judges call competitors out of the line-up in groups of three to five at a time for comparison poses. At this point the top five competitors are chosen and only they are allowed to compete in the final two rounds, which take place in the evening. Round 3 comprises three-minute individual posing routines. In round 4, the competitors are called back out onstage to perform the compulsory poses again. Finally, there is the posedown, a one-minute period during which the finalists strike as many of their best poses as possible. The judges then get together and choose the winner by consensus.

What makes this subjective assessment even more complicated is that, lacking objective measures, judges can only compare competitors against each other. Even if the group of competitors onstage does not offer particularly good examples of a balanced, symmetrical physique, the judges still have to pick a winner. This often sends a confusing message to competitors about what the judges are actually looking for. Linda Wood-Hoyte, a sixty-three-year-old IFBB pro who has been competing for twenty-two years and has also been a national judge since 1992 and an IFBB International judge since 2002 (not to mention a performer in *The Celebration*), describes it this way. "I think being a judge is more difficult than being a competitor. In the pros, there is usually a clear winner. But in the amateurs you often get trapped into picking someone you don't want to pick because there is nowhere else to go. You can only judge what's onstage the day of the contest. Sometimes anything you pick, you lose."

This is especially true when it comes to the women. Female athletes as a whole, and female bodybuilders in particular, have only been seriously training with weights for twenty-five years, which means that no one has any clear idea what women are fully capable of—and therefore no one knows how to establish a standard for a winning female physique. "When it comes to muscularity," explains Wennerstrom, "the implication is that it is masculine simply because most individuals are used to seeing high levels of muscular development only on men. The mainstream population has not been educated to understand or realize women have the capacity to achieve physical development at a very high level."

Over the years, Wennerstrom continues, "controversies have arisen on an almost annual basis due to the level of muscularity the contestants were reaching at the time. The judges found themselves in a very difficult situation when attempting to evolve along with the rapid evolution of muscular development in the competitors. In some ways I feel sorry for the judges. On the other hand, it can be frustrating when there is often a perception that the sport's administrators would want to slow or reverse this inevitable evolutionary process."

For example, when a body like Bev's enters a competition, judges have no frame of reference for what they are seeing. At the competition depicted in *Pumping Iron II*, Bev looked massive and extreme, out of proportion when compared to the other women onstage. Despite the fact that she was undoubtedly the most built bodybuilder, Bev placed eighth. But she raised the bar. Bev established a new standard that female bodybuilders strove to achieve. Judges now had a new definition for the female physique.

That kind of limit-pushing comes at a cost, however.

Invariably, harder, bigger muscles seem to reignite the IFBB's discomfort with the "level of masculinity" displayed by the women. When this happens, they publicly take a stand on femininity, reminding the judges that they are evaluating women, not men. Competitors and judges find themselves asking the same questions they were asking in 1983, namely, how do you judge femininity? With no clear answers, judges tend to mark down for bigness. That is the cycle: grow and retract, grow and retract, grow and retract. Sometimes, when the IFBB is really concerned, they go a step further and rather than just making an announcement, they formally issue a new set of guidelines or send out a letter stating their "new" position.

This happened in 1991 when Bev showed up at the Ms. Olympia contest—the most important competition in pro bodybuilding—and weighed in at 160 pounds, up from 138 pounds the previous year. True to her nature, Bev broke the mold yet again, creating one of the most powerful and extreme physiques seen on a woman to date. Though women's muscularity was trending bigger, there were nevertheless negative perceptions of Bev's look. Witnesses will tell you that Bev was certainly built, but her symmetry was way off. She looked "blocky." Her waist was "thick." She was not "feminine." In that show, Bev came in second, which was close enough to first to make the IFBB nervous.

Following the competition, the IFBB formally issued new guidelines that featured words like "femininity" and cautioned the judges that women shouldn't get "too big." Judges took the guidelines very seriously, and in 1992 big women began losing across the board. Writing in "Judging Procedures in IFBB Women's Bodybuilding: Suggestions and a Warning" about the results of the Jan Tana Classic competition, Dobbins reported, "Anja Schreiner, very attractive but with only a [limited] degree of development, won the Ms. International. Marie-Laure Mahibar, who had worked her way up into the Top 5 at the Ms. Olympia, placed eleventh in the Jan Tana Classic (when she should have gotten first or second)." It got so bad that fans refused to buy tickets to the 1992 Ms. Olympia competition, claiming they didn't want to "witness a beauty contest." (It was just about this time that Laurie decided to create *The Celebration*.) With tickets sales down, the IFBB had to do something, so they changed the guidelines back to the way they had been. Things returned to normal, for the most part.

Until the late 1990s. Ben Weider had been dreaming of the Olympics ever since he and his brother Joe began bodybuilding in the 1950s. He wanted the sport to be recognized by the International Olympic Committee but had been turned down repeatedly. It seemed that alleged drug use was the primary deterrent for the International Olympic Committee. Bodybuilders were generally considered to be drug abusers, and it didn't help the federation's image when a competitor died from an overdose, which is what happened to IFBB pro Andreas Munzer who died just hours after a competition in 1996 when he suffered kidney, liver, and heart failure from taking diuretics. Since the IFBB doesn't routinely test for drugs (testing is costly and often ineffective, since competitors outwit them by tapering off their drug use before a show or simply using newer drugs that don't have tests yet), it was impossible to counter the perception. Especially when it came to the women. Public opinion held that it was impossible for women to get truly big muscles naturally and therefore all very muscular women must be on steroids, but determining whether they actually were or not did not become a priority for the IFBB. In the IFBB's eyes, women bodybuilders with their "extreme, unnatural physiques" were giving the sport a bad name.

Dobbins laments in his article "Professional Bodybuilding for Women: A Victim of Its Own Success," "If the IFBB is so concerned about drugs, it should have instituted a full program of drug testing long ago—and damn the difficulties and expenses. How fair is it to say, 'We are not going to drug test, but we are simply going to assume you are using and abusing anabolic drugs.'"

In the same article, Dobbins describes how rumors started flying that because the International Olympic Committee didn't like "big women," the IFBB was planning to "restructure" the women's division. It didn't seem to matter that IFBB competitors were professionals and would not be the crop of athletes considered for Olympic participation anyway; Olympic candidates would come from the amateur federation closely linked to the IFBB, the National Physique Committee (NPC), which does randomly test for steroids. Regardless, it looked as if the IFBB was going to cut the pro women out altogether, and in late 1999 the Ms. Olympia contest, sponsored by the IFBB, was canceled due to "financial difficulties." There was a huge outcry, and ultimately the show was rescheduled, but fans and competitors felt the IFBB was sending a clear message: the federation wanted to dissociate itself from the women they felt were tarnishing their image and hindering their chance of being officially recognized by the International Olympic Committee.

Since then, the IFBB has made two more official attempts to clean up the ladies' acts. In early 2000, a letter was issued to IFBB competitors from Jim Manion, then chairman of the Professional Judges Committee, in which he wrote: "The following is the criteria by which all IFBB Women bodybuilders will be judged: Full General Assessment—Healthy Appearance, Face, Make-Up, Skin Tone. Symmetry, Presentation, Separations, and Muscularity BUT NOT TO THE EXTREME!" Dobbins responded with an article entitled, "Is the IFBB Turning Women's Bodybuilding into a Beauty Contest?" which asks a host of questions, including, "What do these rules have to do with the sport of bodybuilding?"

The latest mandate was issued in December 2004. Manion, now vice chairman of the IFBB Professional Division, wrote the following mandate to all IFBB female athletes regarding female muscularity:

> For aesthetics and health reasons, the IFBB Professional Division requests that female athletes in Bodybuilding, Fitness and Figure decrease the amount of muscularity by a factor of 20%.
>
> This request for a 20% decrease in the

amount of muscularity applies to those female athletes whose physiques require the decrease regardless of whether they compete in Bodybuilding, Fitness or Figure.

All professional judges have been advised of the proper criteria for assessing female physiques.

A similar mandate was not issued to the men's division.

Fifty-year-old amateur competitor Robin Parker, who has been competing off and on for eighteen years and still has dreams of turning pro (she also performed in *The Celebration*), was all but defeated by the latest news. "I think the twenty percent mandate is ridiculous. I don't understand how they can tell us it is about health. If they really cared about health, then they'd test for diuretics at the shows. And then they might be able to tell us they were concerned about our health and then we might actually believe them. The fact that they haven't said anything to the men is hypocritical and it doesn't make any sense."

Parker described a possible game plan to prepare to become 20 percent smaller: "I would seriously consider not training certain body parts at all and the ones that needed to be brought up, I would train them just a little bit harder. I'd do tons and tons of cardio and basically not eat very much to try to lose mass. But who knows if that would be enough?"

There has been some progress to speak of, however. In the early 1980s, Doris Barrilleaux, then head of female bodybuilding for the IFBB, adapted the sport to the unique needs of the female competitors. Male competitors performed seven compulsory poses: front lat spread, rear lat spread, front double biceps, rear double biceps, side chest, side triceps, abdominal, and thigh. Barrilleaux excluded the front and rear lat spreads from the women's compulsory poses, stating, "I don't like them," and "Women don't have lats anyway." Men pose with a clenched fist, but Barrilleaux recommended that women pose with hands open so that they would look more feminine. Ultimately, this makes posing more difficult because it is far easier to punctuate a pose with tightened fists than with fingers spread wide.

Dobbins took on the IFBB concerning the lat-spread issue long ago, but in 2002 he formally stated his case in his article, "Why No Lat Spread for Women? Because Doris Didn't Like It." "[No lat spread] shows a fundamental disrespect for female bodybuilding. Given that the width, density, and muscularity of the back involves the biggest concentration of muscles in the upper body, ignoring this pose indicates the judges are not interested in judging women's bodybuilding as a real physique contest, but that they are more interested in what is euphemistically called the 'complete package'—meaning an emphasis on conventional beauty, marketability, and sexual attractiveness of the women competitors." After twenty years of debate, the lat spread was finally added to the women's compulsory poses in 2004.

This desire for the marketable "complete package" seems to be at least partially responsible for two new competitive categories that arose for women during the 1990s: Fitness and Figure. Fitness was initially created for women who wanted to compete but didn't want to get big and muscley. Fitness competitors get to wear things like high heels and costumes, perform MTV-esque aerobic routines with back flips, and execute mandatory movements like one-arm push-ups, high kicks, and splits. Ironically, over the years the bodies of many Fitness competitors have evolved to become more muscular, forcing them either to become bodybuilders or to find ways to keep their muscles reasonably sized.

Figure competitors, who are difficult to distinguish from Miss USA contestants, haven't faced that dilemma yet. They come out onstage first in a one-piece swimsuit and later in a bikini, always wear high heels, and stand before the judges performing a series of quarter turns. Show promoters, sponsors, and the media love Fitness and Figure competitors because they seem to embody the popular notion of "ultimate femininity" and believe people will pay to see them compete. It didn't take long before the sponsorship dollars, prize money, and press coverage that used to rain down on female bodybuilders began to deluge Fitness and Figure competitors, leaving female bodybuilders with virtually no exposure at all.

Yet the elusive "complete package" remains the Holy Grail in women's bodybuilding. Wood-Hoyte doesn't find the standard an unfair measure. She comes from a lifetime in corporate America and feels that her business background gives her a unique perspective. "This is a business. It isn't a charity," she explains. "The IFBB has to walk a fine line between the athletes and what is acceptable for the public, keeping the sport viable and earning some money. I think a lot of change, right or wrong, has to do with trying to get support for the sport. Now you can say that is wrong, but if you don't do something you're going to lose your sponsorship.

"[When I am judging] I always give competitors feedback at the end of the show, and they either choose to listen or they don't. A package has to set the standard. That's what you aim at. As a woman, you have a choice: you either stay in it because you love it, or, if you don't like the standards being set, you may have to drop out."

6

The Celebration: Act I, Scene 3

I had a show to create. And a job to find. The job part would be easy. Even though I loathed the idea, waiting tables would tide me over. It was the show that now officially had me worried.

As soon as I got home from my meeting with Laurie, I began to set up my own little production office in the small room I rented, which had once been the summer porch of the old farmhouse. It was a skeleton scantily dressed in hand-me-down furniture with a stained aqua plush area rug that covered most of the painted gray hard-wood floor, a standing mirror, a table with cast-iron legs I used as my desk, a wardrobe rack where clothes hung exposed, stacked wooden fruit crates for folded things, and a mattress that lay like an island on the floor. The room was cheap because it was drafty. Three of the walls were mostly windows. The bottom half of those walls was wood paneling and that's where I began to tack up the glossies of the women that Laurie had given me—one was even signed for me, "To Kristin, thanks for your help." The fourth wall connected the room to the main house by way of a glass-paned door that led into the kitchen. On that wall I tacked up calendar pages for the months of September, October, and November, circling the date of *The Celebration*—November 5 —in red pen. It was official. Forty-two days. I also taped together two pieces of paper and tacked them up horizontally. I drew a long line across and made twenty-five little marks on the line. Below each mark would be the name and theme of each performer. There was my show, to be determined.

Six weeks. Shit.

I plunked myself down in the sea of photos, essays, and participant information Laurie had loaded me down with. Female musings shouted up from the pages, claiming a bold story of womanhood. Included in the stack were Laurie's own essays on modern Amazons and pieces by Maya Angelou, Lucille Clifton, and even Anne Rice, with titles like "A Woman Is Not a Potted Plant" and "Homage to my Hips." Alice Walker insisted in the opening stanza of her poem "On Stripping Bark from Myself":

> *Because women are expected*
> *to keep silent about*
> *their close escapes*
> *I will not keep silent*
> *and if I am destroyed (naked tree!) someone will*
>   *please*
> *mark the spot*
> *where I fall and know I could not live*
> *silent in my own lies*
> *hearing their "how* nice *she is!"*
> *whose adoration of the retouched image*
> *I so despise.*

Writing like this always got me riled up when I read it in college, not because it was a story that I, at twenty-three, thought I identified with but because it seemed so irreverent, so rebellious. It made me want to shout, "Yeah!

Yeah! I'm not going to be silent either!" What a close escape was, I didn't exactly know. But I thought it was cool that as a rule she didn't want to be *nice*. I'd never thought of that.

Bits and pieces of *The Celebration* flashed in my mind. I lay back on my bed trying to imagine how the whole thing would turn out. I pictured a single spotlight on a dressed-in-black actress reciting Alice Walker's poem before introducing the next act. Then I saw Norman Rockwell's poster of the scrawny little boy standing before a Mr. Atlas poster and wondered what image we could use for a girl. Was there one? Could we use the same Mr. Atlas poster? Could we start the show with that? A nice little homey scene, a bedroom, cozy lighting, a girl longing to have muscles, in front of her mirror?

Or was it loud? Like an announcer for a boxing match. Dimly lit, a microphone hanging from overhead, a long, slow drone, "Laaaadies aaaand Gentlemeeeen! Welcome to *The Celebration of the Most Awesome Female in the Woorrllldddd!*"

No. Not wrestling. Wrong scenario. Something more cutting. A farce. Laurie wanted to make a statement, didn't she? We could have an auction. Or a pre-show auction. With an auction block. And an auctioneer. Because didn't these women, in essence, have to sell themselves to win? Prepare their bodies for speculation? Their bodies a product? She would come out onstage, a man in drag, dressed in a hula skirt and coconut boobs. Everyone would laugh. Funny. It would be funny. A put-on. The whole thing a sham. And the audience would be buying it. They would get into the bidding. People yelling, "I'll take her for five thousand!" Maybe I could actually get paid.

No. Might be too brash. Flowers. Cycles of flowers. Growing things. Things that grow naturally. What we do to make ourselves grow. All the things we do to make ourselves something other than what we are. Bodybuilders, supplements, fake boobs, hair dye, fake nails. Everyone does it. Funny. It could be funny. Comediennes making a flower grow with fake nails and protein powder.

Or something like that. I didn't know. God, I didn't know what to write. I sat back up and shuffled through the photos around me. The women smiled up at me from the 8-by-10's, striking peacock poses, shying away from nothing that the eye could see. Pride and determination radiated from their faces, the only things tangibly human about their bodies. Below, in barely there bikinis, warriors flexed their biceps, spread their lats, and imposed their glutes. "How do they do that?" I wondered. "Why do they do that?" It was one thing to be sporty, but something else entirely to cultivate a physique like that. Their bodies looked like suits of armor, their faces pleased with the power and protection they provided. I closed my eyes, picked a picture at random, and made my first phone call. Dawn Whitham answered.

"I'm calling my performance the White Lace Affair," she told me.

"I'm sorry?" The phone slipped from the cradle I'd created between my head and shoulder.

"White Lace Affair. I want to show people that you can have it all. You know, you can be muscular and big and still hot." Dawn spoke rapidly. Her voice swayed up at the end of each sentence, making most statements sound like questions.

"Mmmm. Interesting." Hot. She wanted to be hot. I looked at her photo. Taken at a competition, it showed her with her chest puffed proudly, arms crooked at the elbow, fists dug in at her waist. Teased brown hair stood straight up, a cocklike comb above her forehead; the rest was pulled back in a tight braid that curled around her neck and rested on her chest. And what a chest! Pectoral muscles rose vehemently, dramatically dropping like a steep cliff into the center cleft, giving cleavage an entirely new definition. A teeny fuchsia bikini top desperately clung to the round breasts that looked like an afterthought, strategically placed atop the plateau of pecs.

"I'm a do-everything kind of person, you know? If there were forty hours in a day I'd want to do more. So I won't really need much help with White Lace. I've got it all planned out. See, I'm gonna start wearing, like, a white posing suit with a black jacket and tails. You know, it'll look like a tux."

"Uh-huh." Light blue eye shadow glowed above her eyes.

"The first part'll be slow and sensual, kind of like a sexy ballet. And then, bang! I pull off the jacket and you'll see my white sequin thong posing suit and white lace garter. And I'll start hitting these hot poses. It'll be sexy and powerful."

"Yeah, sounds like it. Sounds like you've really thought it through." I didn't know how to respond to this. I changed the topic.

"Do you mind if I ask you a few questions?"

"Go for it."

Dawn rattled through answers to the list of questions I'd planned to ask all the participants about their background, how they got into bodybuilding, what ideas they had for their performance and what props, lighting, and so forth were needed. She was bubbly and helpful and finished every fourth or fifth sentence with, "You know what I'm sayin'?"

Dawn was in her early thirties and had previously been an eighty-pound anorectic long-distance runner and self-proclaimed control freak. She channeled her controlling nature in a positive direction and began lifting weights, found it easy to gain bulk, and fell in love with the look. One hundred pounds and 500 cc breast implants later (giving her approximately a D-cup), Dawn found herself placing well in competitions, but not placing in the Top 5. Judges told her that her look was perfect, but her breast implants were too big. "So, you're telling me that because my boobs are too big I'm not a Top Five finisher?" she would ask. "Well, no, not exactly," they would respond. She would fight with them about what the right size of breasts was, exactly, and found that flat-chested and big-breasted women alike were not considered winning material. Neither was considered an example of perfect symmetry.

"I'm not a real good game player," she said. "What you see is what you get. I'm up-front with people and am not going to walk around and kiss their butts. You know what I'm sayin'? Competing is all about playing the game. It's not how you look, but how you play it. It really puts me out."

She considered herself an extremist and speculated that all bodybuilders are into being different or extreme in some way. "It takes a lot to go the distance, to get yourself to look this way. And you have to be strong to be able to accept the way people react to you." Dawn enjoyed a wide range of reactions, from Asian tourists who said they loved the look and wanted their picture taken with her to men who were rude and said mean things to her in public. A part of her got off on the attention—whether positive or negative—because at the end of the day she never wanted to be the person in the crowd whom nobody noticed. Most of the time she could hack it, but there were days when, say, she just wanted to go to the Stop 'n' Shop and get some half-and-half for her coffee, when a person with a pointing finger and an "Oh my god look at her!" would tick her off. "I don't get pissed about what I've done to my body. I get pissed about how unintelligent people can be reacting to it. You'd think by now the world could accept that everybody is different, but people are afraid to be different. At least allow others the freedom to push their own boundaries. You know what I'm sayin'?"

On the train ride home I'd constructed a final question to cut through the insidious intricacies of persona. If I had to help these women reveal the essence of their being and express the true voice of female power, then I first had to find it. Without actually seeing them until two days before the show, I realized I'd have to glean their core by phone. My question had to elicit the most honest of answers, compelling each interviewee to reveal an aspect of herself that even she rarely glimpsed. I'd gotten the idea for the question from my conversation with Laurie when she explained that I had to help the women transmit the magic of their femaleness. The question: "What is your femaleness?"

"Well," responded Dawn, "it's like I said. Everyone thinks having muscles destroys your femininity, and it doesn't. My muscles make me hot." Being hot was her femaleness. "But femaleness and strength is not just a physical thing. It's a combination. Mostly it's just something you are. I'm very independent, smart, and business-like. I have a career. I'm a personal trainer. I can bench four hundred pounds and fix my own car. I also ride a Harley. Sexy things and the mind can go together, too. Sexy is powerful, too.

"Anyway," she moved on, "in my performance I want it to look soft at first, kind of like fog or smoke. You can get a smoke machine, can't you? And I'll need a white chair and a wood window."

"A smoke machine?" There was no way. The last time I'd seen a smoke machine was in high school at the battle-of-the-bands when Tommy Hamilton's band was trying to be Van Halen.

"Yeah. And the window has to be white. In the first part, it'll be like I'm looking out the window."

"I don't know if a smoke machine will really give the dramatic effect you want." While I had to agree with her sexy-smarts-strength connection in theory, I really wasn't prepared for lace garters and hot posing routines. "Dawn, has Laurie talked to you about what the show is about?"

"Yeah, and I think it's a great idea."

"So you know that *The Celebration* is all about breaking barriers, right? About depicting bodybuilding not just as a muscle sport, but as an art form? And that all the pieces should be about strength and independence?"

"Yeah. What Laurie is doing is awesome. I'm an artist, too. My mom was a ballet dancer so I've been around the-ater and art and stuff, so I love the fact that Laurie is pro-moting female bodybuilders in an artistic light."

"Yeah, it's great. Definitely. Great. Do me a favor, will you? Maybe give some thought to a backup plan, you know, in case this doesn't really fit in the greater scheme of the show. Maybe think about your favorite heroine. We could adapt her to the stage and you could play her."

"Oh, that's okay. I've already got this choreographed and everything."

"Okay. Just something to think about in case we have to make some changes."

Hot. She wanted to be hot. Who was I to say that wasn't her true inner nature? What was I supposed to do as a director? Make her hotter? Advise for red lighting rather than pink? I didn't know what to do. Wasn't I supposed to come up with new images of female strength? On my performance list I wrote "White Lace Affair" with a question mark next to it. I pictured the dressed-in-black actress reciting Alice Walker:

> . . . *mark the spot*
> *where I fall and know I could not live*
> *silent in my own lies*
> *hearing their "how* nice *she is!"*
> *whose adoration of the retouched image*
> *I so despise.*

[Pause]

*Ladies and Gentlemen, it's my pleasure to intro-
duce the next performer, Dawn Whitham in the
White Lace Affair!"*

They didn't exactly go together. And a smoke machine?
There was no way. But I'd have to solve all that later. I had
women to call. Twenty-four of them. So I made the next
call and then the next one.

Days passed. I left messages. No one called me back.
Finally, a voice answered. A deep voice.

"Hello?"

"Hi, I'm calling for Colleene Colley."

"Yes."

"May I please speak with her?"

"Honey, this is Colleene. I know this lovely voice
sounds like a man's, but I am very much a woman. How
can I help you?"

Colleene's voice was commanding and warm. She was
quick to joke and her Southern charms put me at ease.

"Sure, I'm comin'. I'm not sure what you're goin' to do
with the likes of me, though. I mean I'm not a bodybuilder or anything. I'm an athlete. People like to watch
bodybuilders. That's entertainment. Gives them some-

thing to talk about. What I do is technical. I mean, you're either a fan of weightlifting, or you're not."

Colleene was training to be on the first women's Olympic lifting team to compete in the games. Women's weightlifting wasn't yet an official sport in 1993, but it was ultimately introduced in 1996, in time for Sydney in 2000. Colleene had been a pioneer competing against boys at the age of fifteen in 1980 in Georgia. She beat them, but felt guilty because she knew they were humiliated to be beaten by a girl. She started training with weights to make herself stronger for basketball, but found she had a natural gift for lifting, a gift that wasn't nurtured at her own school. She had to go to a gym twenty-three miles away to train because when she went into the weight room at her high school, the boys' weightlifting coach eyed her and warned, "I hope you don't plan on lifting any weight." By 1993 Colleene had already won ten national titles and three world championships.

I looked down at her picture. Steely determination fixed her eyes on a distant horizon; her teeth were bared. A thin film of white chalk splotched her trunklike body; veins spread wildly over up-stretched arms, the barbell looking powerless above her. It was as if she'd just wrestled a planet and was about to throw it deep into space.

"What I do is lift really heavy weight over my head very quickly. Our technique is so defined and specific that if you're off one-tenth of a centimeter it'll screw up your whole lift. It's like using a power jack for a car. You put that baby in a specific place and you can lift the front end of your car, you put her in the wrong place you're not going to lift anything, you'll snap that tire jack in half."

I was trying to picture a quick transition between performances, stagehands taking down Dawn's white window and then hauling hundred-pound weights onstage in less than ten seconds. "How much do you plan to lift for the show?"

"I'll do a snatch. That's when you lift the weight from the floor to overhead in one continuous motion, at one hundred and eighty-eight pounds. I'll do that in about three to four seconds. Then I'll do a clean and jerk at about two hundred and twenty pounds. That's when you lift the barbell first to your chin, and then above your head. That lift takes about six to eight seconds. And darlin', I'll be setting a national record with that lift for my hundred-thirty-two-pound weight class, so get ready to pop that champagne backstage."

I was scribbling down the details.

"But, like I said, people are either into the sport or

they're not. Crowds love bodybuilding, though. I tried my hand at it for a few shows. I even won Overall at the Southern States Bodybuilding Competition, but I couldn't take the discipline. I have plenty of drive to train that hard, plenty of drive to lift and be at the gym all the time and do cardio, but I'll be the first to admit that I just do not have the willpower to leave food alone long enough to keep my body fat down. Food was on my mind twenty-four/seven. Every waking moment I was thinking about food, what my body was burning, what it looked like, what might be making me hold too much water, or making me constipated. It's a self-centered total obsession, one that I admire and loathe all at the same time, mind you. But all that to be onstage for ninety seconds? Not for me. I love food too much. Hell, I'm raised in the South. Here food is entertainment."

"Listen, I have one more question for you."

"What's that, honey?"

"I'm trying to get to the essence of the show. You know, Laurie's vision for this production is to celebrate women's strength in all forms."

"I know, I think it's a fabulous idea."

"It is, it is. It's so great to be working on it. Anyway, I'm trying to get to the core of who all the women are, to understand what they pride themselves on as women. So here's my question: What do you consider your femaleness?"

"My what?"

"You know, what makes you feel you are who you are, but as a woman." Trying to articulate what femaleness was sounded stupid. I didn't even know.

"Good God, girl, I have no idea what you are talking about," she said and laughed. "Look, I have always been an athlete, and I love sports. I love the competition of myself with myself, testing myself and my capabilities. It is an amazing thing to push your body and mind to the limit. I don't care if you're male or female; it's an amazing thing just knowing you can do it. I love being a strong woman, mentally and physically. It's who I am and who I always will be. I don't know if that answers your question or not."

"It certainly does. Thanks for your time."

"My pleasure, sugar."

More calls, more answering machines. Days passed . . . a week or so. Three times I got through. There was the woman who wanted to be Little Red Riding Hood and eat the wolf. And then there was the Biker Chick who wanted to beat up two guys. And a Miss America who wanted to tear off her gown. All wanted smoke machines.

Standing before my show chart with twenty spots empty and five filled in—White Lace Affair, Red Riding Hood, Biker Chick, Stripping Miss America, Lifter—I began to wonder was this really the voice of female power? Did stripping constitute strength? Could men be in the show even if they did get beat up? Could Alice Walker and the White Lace Affair come one right after the other?

This was not what I expected.

Four weeks. I hadn't written a word.

"It's okay. It's okay." I stood in front of my mirror talking to myself. "I can figure this out. This is my Broadway debut. I *will* figure this out." But my eyes looked round with fear. "Stop it!" I took a deep breath, rolled my head around, moved my jaw, shook my arms out, and set my eyes squarely upon myself. "I am a director." I squinted my eyes, tilted my forehead down slightly, trying to look unwavering. "You will help them create images of strength that have never been seen before. Your job is to stretch them. To push them. People resist change. They'll want to do what's easiest. You can do it. They can do it. It will be done."

I wondered what it felt like to be them. Puffing my chest up, holding my arms bowed out to each side, I walked to and from the mirror as if my body moved in two parts, twisting my whole upper torso from the waist. I flexed one nearly nonexistent bicep, and then the other, striking a double-biceps pose. I was impervious to resistance.

And then the phone rang. It was Laurie wanting to know how it was going.

I watched myself twirling the phone cord talking to her, telling her that it was all going well except that no one was returning my phone calls and that yes, in fact, the writing was flowing and sure, I'd love to show her, maybe not tomorrow, but the next day and that was good anyway because there were a few inconsistencies I wanted to discuss with her, all the while glancing at the glossies of the women that looked like a chorus tacked up behind me, thinking, "Shit. Oh, shit."

7

What It's Like to Be a Female Bodybuilder

---

etting ready for a competition feels like looking forward to Christmas. At least it does for twenty-nine-year-old amateur competitor Sheila Bleck. It takes her twelve weeks of serious preparation to get ready for a show. Anticipation of the payoff makes her feel giddy, like wondering what presents will be under the Christmas tree, or even better, like falling in love. It's not all about winning, although that would be nice. It's about wondering how far she can push her body. It's about yearning for the hallowed state that all the training and dieting and days of deprivation deliver her to. She can hardly wait until those moments before the show when her body and mind are as finely tuned as an orchestra.

That's why she chooses not to pay attention to what the judges say or the swings in opinion about whether women should sculpt their bodies bigger or smaller. Sheila prefers to feel "in love" and hates it when people "bitch" about the politics of the sport. All that talk ruins it. For her, it's about achieving Zen in the art of body sculpting; manipulating her workout and food intake— carbohydrates, protein, and water—on an almost hourly basis to create the perfect balance between bulk, hardness, and symmetry in time for her ninety seconds onstage. For this, she gives up everything.

"I can't even tell you how lonely my life is. Everybody I know is out clubbing, they're barbecuing, camping, partying. Not me. I'm either at home, at work, or at the gym." But Sheila is clear about her choice. "It's my life. I realize that I'm giving myself something that no one in the world can take away from me. Basically, it was not easy growing up. A lot was taken away. It seems that it's easy for people to rip something out from under you that you care about so much. So when you start gaining something you hold on to it with everything you've got."

What this means is that Sheila's father abandoned the family when she was very young. Her mother worked and was not around to see what happened to Sheila and her twin sister—namely, that certain family members took advantage of the situation. "You only have to let your mind go to understand what I'm saying," she explained. "There was no one to trust. So you see where I come from."

Where she came from compels Sheila to wake up at 4 A.M. six days a week to go to the gym and do cardio before going to her factory job. She returns to the gym after work to lift for an hour, and if she's getting ready for a show, she'll practice posing for another hour after that. She's been doing this for ten years and wouldn't change one minute of it. Everybody in the gym talks to Sheila to say hi, get training advice, or wish her luck for an upcoming show. She talks very quickly and enthusiastically and with the authority of someone who has banished bullshit from her life. She gets to the point, is happy to help, but won't tolerate it if someone is just pumping her for information without giving her something in return. It's not that she actually wants something specific; she just doesn't want to feel like someone is feeding off the focus and knowledge she's worked so hard to cultivate. When she senses that this happening, she doesn't want anything further to do with that person.

I thought Sheila had pinned a guy when I went to Gold's Gym to tag along during her workout, but she was just adjusting his spine while he lay facedown on the floor. Watching her work out made me feel like a complete schlub. Her skin was tanned and luminous. It had a presence unto itself, reminding me that the skin is actually a body organ. Compared to hers, most people's skin resembled play dough thumbed over their skeletons, but Sheila's seemed to live and breathe independently. It participated in her workout, stretching and contracting, making room for her muscles and veins as she heaved the weights.

When she looks at herself, she doesn't see shoulders, arms, legs, a back, and a stomach. Sheila sees each and every muscle and makes sure to work each and every one of them separately. When I said, "Wow, your shoulders are huge," Sheila explained that a shoulder is actually made up of four strips of muscle—the interior and exterior deltoid, the biceps, and the triceps. She demonstrated various shoulder lifts, each time bending from her upper waist at varying degrees, saying, "See? See that one there.

Look at it pop. I mean, sure, I could lift a ton of weight if I wanted to, but it's not about that. It's more about sculpting each and every muscle." Sheila began to seem like one of those clear plastic biology statues from science class that enable you to see right though the myriad layers of muscle and bone and veins and organs. She seemed like a highly efficient machine, until she said something like, "People don't know how to react to me. They don't know what to do. They stumble. And it's like, 'Why are you acting that way? If you act like that then I get uncomfortable and then I get embarrassed and if I get embarrassed I get upset and then I'm going to leave.'"

Sheila is lucky because she has the right genetics. In bodybuilding it's all about genetics—without the right ones, you have to work that much harder to build muscle, or take drugs to add bulk, or just plain face the fact that you will never win. You are secretly happy if you have good genetics because that means you have what it takes to create the type of physique judges are looking for. It's sort of like if you knew you had the "popular" gene when you went to high school, then you wouldn't have to worry about not fitting in. Sheila has a naturally tapered V shape. She has a long torso and long limbs with naturally small joints that act as punctuation points for full and rounded muscles. She has no difficulty adding bulk. In fact, she has to be careful not to gain too much. Add to that the fact that once upon a time Sheila was a dancer and loves music, which in her case means that she is very flexible and moves through her poses with ease and grace. *Women's Physique World* says she has "pro" written all over her.

Sheila keeps her body fat at about 8 percent off-season, which is unusual. Most competitors gain twenty to forty pounds and then have the daunting task of losing it before a show. They start preparing twelve weeks out. Since Sheila keeps herself in good shape year-round she really only has to start focusing about eight weeks out. But once she does, it gets intense.

For the first four weeks she cuts out things like mustard and fat-free dressing from her diet, all the little extra calories that get overlooked. She figures these account for an easy three hundred calories a day. She has a protein drink for breakfast with two scoops of protein powder, one teaspoon of flax-seed oil, and one teaspoon of milk thistle. She wants to stay away from sugar so she doesn't even eat a banana. Morning snack is a protein bar. For lunch she has half a pound of ground turkey breast with seasoning, a third of a sweet potato, and maybe some cabbage. Her afternoon snack is another protein drink and for dinner she has what she had for lunch. She wakes up at midnight because she's hungry, and eats egg whites with green onion—when she's really hungry she'll eat as many as ten egg whites.

She hits the gym twice a day and after lifting she practices her freestyle routine and compulsory poses in front of a mirror. Posing is a workout all by itself because you are holding still for thirty seconds in an unnatural position, making your muscles as hard as you can, and trying to breathe all at the same time. Posing helps to harden and accentuate the striations in the muscle, which is desirable because it is another way to show detailed definition. A good way to tell if you're in good posing shape is to hold an ab pose while talking and breathing at the same time. You try it—place your hands behind your head, point one toe out in front of you, crunch your abs together with all your might but keep your chest up so that people can see your "six pack" (which you know is in there somewhere), and hold this for sixty seconds and carry on a casual conversation with someone. If you can do this without gasping, you deserve to be impressed with yourself.

During those first four weeks Sheila might tweak her diet a bit if she's not getting results. Her calorie expenditure may be the same, but she might jack the protein or the carbohydrates higher to shock her body into doing something she wants, like lose weight. When I met Sheila, her body was being stubborn and refused to lose two pounds. She started her training at 167 pounds and was 163 at week 6, but she wanted to be 160 or 161. So she and her coach—she has a trainer, as many body-builders do—were manipulating her carbs, jacking them up high one day and then dropping them low the next. It's like being on a wacky roller-coaster ride. On the high-carb day she has tons of energy, but the next day when she deprives herself, her energy will plummet; and then the next day she'll kick it back up again, which gives her a rush. She loves the ride, especially when she can feel her water weight lessening, her fat cells shrinking, and her muscle bellies—the full area of the muscle—getting harder. She loves waking up after a high-carb day to see her veins looking like hoses (a state also known as increased vascularity). Pumping carbs into your system after being deprived of them pumps everything up and she wakes with her entire venal system looking like an interconnected highway across her body. She describes this state with bedazzled eyes: "It's just freakish. That's pretty much when you look the best."

During the final four weeks leading up to the show, Sheila maintains her weight at 160 pounds. Her ultimate goal is to lose three additional pounds of water weight right before the show, which will bring her in at 157 pounds. Her coach doesn't want her to come in any lower, not even 156—it's that precise—because he's worried she'll look dry, which tends to fall into the category of unfeminine. You end up looking super-gaunt, too much like stone with skin stretched over you.

In the last four weeks, Sheila cuts the protein drink and bar from her diet. She will eat five to six meals a day of either egg whites with one whole egg and any vegetable she wants (cauliflower is preferable because it doesn't leave her gassy) or chicken breast, a little sweet potato, and whatever vegetable she wants. Sometimes she'll swap out chicken with fish—a pound of sole on the barbecue with lemon juice. At this point she has to vary her protein sources, otherwise she gets diarrhea.

The last ten days Sheila cuts out eggs and salt and tries to eat only fish. No vegetables because they give her gas. It's just fish and sweet potatoes. Water intake is one to two gallons a day, to flush her system. The only thing she does do which she shouldn't (except for sometimes sneaking a glass of Crystal Light or a package of Sweet 'n'

Low) is drink a cup of coffee in the morning. If she didn't, she would lose her mind.

The Monday and Tuesday before the show are the hardest. Carbs are eliminated completely. She doesn't go anywhere because she's too tired and doesn't have any energy to do anything except sleep. She wakes up to go to the bathroom, eat, pose, and maintain her water intake. Anytime she feels anything like weight on her body she poses, and she keeps posing until she thinks she sees a change, until the muscle looks harder in the guilty area.

During this time Sheila feels untouchable, as if she's floating out of this world, and also as if she could cry. She's very emotional and loves everyone but also realizes how profound the world really is. She can't sleep very long, because she's in a weird twilight zone and is wired and sleepy all at the same time; not to mention that she is monitoring the water and food situation hourly. If she's not peeing at least every twenty to thirty minutes, she makes sure to increase her water intake. And she poses.

By Wednesday, Sheila starts to bring the carbs back in a little bit. By Thursday, she brings the water down to one gallon. She's adding more carbs—a small portion of sweet potato every other hour. On alternate hours she eats protein. On Friday, Sheila eats the most delicious orange she has ever eaten in her whole life. And then she eats half a sweet potato every other hour, alternating with protein. Water is down to half a gallon a day. It's all about water depletion and carb infusion. If she feels shrink-wrapped and can't think, then she's in great shape.

When Saturday finally arrives, Sheila is having a complete out-of-body experience, except that all she feels is her body. She is happy. She has butterflies. She wants to kiss everyone. She eats sweet potatoes. She loves hanging out with the other women backstage and doesn't experience the bitter competition that most competitors complain about because she feels she isn't competing against anyone but herself. "I'm the one that's in control of what I'm doing on that stage. Bodybuilding doesn't control me. The judges are in control of what they're in control of, but that's their problem, not mine. And I'm not going to let it be my problem. I know what I am. I know who I am. I know where I came from and I'm not going to forget it. That's what needs to be remembered. If you start worrying about what everyone else says, you're going to be falling on your face."

The one thing that Sheila does hate about waiting backstage is all the Fitness and Figure competitors chatting and fixing their hair and actually eating. Female bodybuilders have to wait backstage while Fitness and Figure competitions happen, delirious hours while Figure competitors make endless series of quarter turns.

And then the female bodybuilders are called out. In the five minutes of prejudging, the judges call out competitor numbers and compare them against each other. By the end of the second round the judges have chosen five finalists to return for the evening show. For everyone else it is over. There will be no ninety seconds of performing their routine. It is over. For this reason Sheila finds bodybuilding heartbreaking: all that work to stand in front of a panel of judges who pick you apart in just a few minutes. And if you have bad genetics, you never even stand a chance.

But Sheila can't imagine doing anything else. "I don't have anything else to believe in. This is the most positive thing that's ever happened to me, and I have given my whole life to it. I have been doing it for half of my lifetime and it's scary to think about stepping out because it would be like stepping into a life I don't know."

8

The Celebration: Act II, Scene 1

What I didn't know was how I was going to break it to Laurie that the show wasn't exactly shaping up the way she had envisioned.

When I arrived at her place for our meeting, the production office could no longer pass as an apartment. Business was operating at full throttle. The front door had been left slightly open so that arriving visitors could let themselves in. Paper was everywhere. Where small piles had once littered the place, tall stacks now towered precariously. A small bump could send whatever order had been established in the stack swirling to the floor. I was worried I'd be the culprit, so I stayed by the door. Michelle, the administrative assistant, sat at a desk constructed from a card table and nodded hello while she talked into the receiver wedged between her shoulder and ear and stamped envelopes. Another woman, fortyish, with rich red hair and a round freckled face, had commandeered the bed and was flipping through papers, occasionally yanking one from the pile. She called across the room and introduced herself as Cecilia, one of the actresses in the show and a close friend of Laurie's.

"Good. You two have met." Laurie walked sideways through the maze of her flat from the kitchen, a chicken breast in one hand and a bottle of water in the other. It amazed me that her big bowed arms managed never to knock anything over. "Cecilia is interested in being the assistant director. You could use some help, couldn't you?" Before I could respond with much more than a "Sure, I guess that's okay" smile, Laurie continued: "She's taking acting classes at the Henry Street Settlement, and she's recruited her friends from class to be the actresses. Her daughter goes to the School for the Performing Arts. Bridgett is one of the teenage girls I was telling you about.

She is going to be in the show, isn't she, Cecilia? I hope its okay with you. I'd really like to get her involved."

Between bites, Laurie launched into the list of things I just was not going to believe were happening. More money had been donated, photographers were giving freely of their time to create a book, and a Broadway producer whose husband was a famous Broadway dancer had caught wind of *The Celebration* and wanted to lend her assistance. "She'll be here in fifteen minutes! She just called, and I told her you were coming. She wants to hear your ideas. Can you believe it? This is getting so big!"

No. I couldn't believe it. My ideas weren't exactly stellar, not to mention that the little question of vision needed to be addressed, but I have a funny reflex when I am overwhelmed. I tend to look placid and talk as if I am confident. One part of me must be stalling while the other part tries to figure out what to do. Laurie had a way of piling on so many things at once that I often ended up stuck in management mode while the rest of me was trying desperately not to panic. From the outside it must have looked as if I was taking it all in stride. At the time, I was also calculating how often a young theater wannabe gets to tell her ideas to a Broadway producer, and I figured that it must not be often at all, so I had to just go for it. That's the blessing and curse of being twenty-three.

I carefully made my way to the bed, where Laurie, Cecilia, Mr. Kitty, and I arranged ourselves. I had constructed a little speech about the incongruities of White Lace and Alice Walker, which, at that moment, completely escaped me, because I was racking my brain to come up with a plan for the show to tell the producer. Instead of my speech, all I could think to tell Laurie was, "I think we have some problems." I divulged the themes I'd collected thus far. An odd smile grew on her face as I was speaking.

"I'm not surprised. There's a side to this I should tell you about." She looked from Cecilia back to me, weighing whether she should disclose the secret. Cecilia seemed to watch Laurie's every move.

"And that is?" I couldn't imagine.

"Well, a large number of these women, aside from the competitive circuit, wrestle men for a living. They get paid thousands of dollars to put men in compromising positions." I must have looked shocked because she quickly added. "It's not sexual. Well, not overtly anyway. They make videos of these sessions and then sell them. They can make ten thousand dollars for one video. So it doesn't surprise me that some of the performances are a little sexy. I'll show you. I've got one."

It was a homemade, handheld video. There was a man's voice and a woman's legs. The woman was sitting on a couch.

Man's voice: "Gee, Cara, I wonder what would happen if I put my head between those thighs of yours?" [camera zooms in closer to the massive thighs.] "Those are some pretty amazing thighs you have there. You wouldn't hurt me if I put my head in there, would you?"

Woman's voice: "I don't know, Tony, why don't you give it a try?" [A man's head comes into view and he places it between her thighs. Slowly, the thighs close on him, tighter and tighter, her muscles flexing and bulging, his eyes doing the same.]

Man's voice: [breathlessly.] "Wow, Cara. You're amazing."

The buzzer buzzed and Laurie reentered the maze to retrieve the producer from the hallway. "Pretty wild stuff, huh?" She clicked off the VCR as she left, her laugh trailing behind her. I sat staring at the TV, trying to determine what to do with the information, wondering whether or not she'd addressed my concern.

Cecilia began bubbling over about what an amazing

woman Laurie was, how intelligent and inspirational and how the show was going to be just amazing. Cecilia tended to co-opt Laurie's lingo. She looked to Laurie like a beacon. In the few minutes that we waited, I learned that Cecilia was a single mother and she wasn't a body-builder but had started boxing (which she loved) and her actress friends were very excited to get started and did I have a script ready to show them? She wanted to help in any way she could. I was nodding at her, thinking, "Great, a gaggle of middle-aged women who took up acting to express themselves. Just what the show needs." I was also breathing deeply to calm my thumping heart. Laurie and the producer were making their way toward us.

The producer was forty or fifty, I couldn't be sure, with long, bleached straw-blond hair that was tied in a pony-tail high on top of her head. She wore a loosely woven black knit sweater, no bra, serious red lipstick, and multi-colored reading glasses that sat on the tip of her nose. "So you're the new talent," she said, shaking my hand. She moved pillows out of the way to make room for herself on the bed. "Tell me what you have in mind."

"Well, I haven't talked this over with Laurie yet, but—"

"Oh, it's okay." Laurie waved her hand. She remained standing, and despite the fact that she was short, she still looked like a giant in a too-small apartment. "Go on. She can help us with anything."

My mind was reeling from the new information, which made my epic of female strength feel even more like a paper cut-out doll whose cut-out clothes were missing. Sure, I had the lingerie outfit, and the Miss America outfit, and the Little Red Riding Hood outfit, but I hadn't exactly found the Strong Woman outfit. But maybe it didn't matter. Maybe no one would really notice. Maybe the producer would just see what I had done with the literature adaptations and marvel and comment on how I managed to marry such a range of voices. Maybe she would look back on that day and tell my future biographer, "I knew from the moment she opened her mouth that the girl had something special." And so I began.

"I want to start with the girls. We have teenage actresses. I want them to be lifting weights, dreaming of being strong, wondering if it is cool. Think Norman Rockwell. Meanwhile, lights will come up on a wall of bodybuilders behind them, kind of like history, like the women who have come before them and made their road easier." I described how the show would work: performer, poetry, performer, dramatic reading, performer, comedienne, and so forth. I couldn't bear to tell her about the

White Lace Affair, but I described the rest. I described the pre-show auction. She sat across from me, silent, hands folded, looking at me over the top of her glasses. She only said one word during my presentation. The only word she uttered was "Comediennes?" This single word accompanied by the deeply skeptical tone that New Yorkers have made synonymous with the phrase "Whaddaya stupid?" was enough to trip me up. I stumbled and stuttered through the rest of my pitch. Her raised eyebrow and repeated eye blinking proved too much for me, and I finished with a question mark in my voice. The producer looked at me for a moment over the top of her glasses, kind of smiled, and said, "Cute." That was it.

Everyone was quiet except for Michelle, who was booking twenty rooms at the Howard Johnson's.

Cecilia gave me a wink of approval.

Laurie broke the silence, eyeing the producer, watching her reaction. "I think I see it. I don't think the auction is really going to work. The women won't think its funny. They'll think you're making fun of them. But the rest of it, you certainly got it all in there." The producer's face told Laurie that she clearly had no idea what she was talking about.

"No, no, no. Wait a minute." She looked incredibly

weary. "Your audience doesn't want poetry. They don't want comediennes. These people want skin, they want muscles, they want it hot, and they want it oiled. They're paying for bodies. *Bam!*" she said, striking her hand and causing her bangles to clash. "That curtain goes up, and I want a wall of bodies, bright lights, music pumping. None of this poetry in between. Your audience won't go for this. This isn't downtown performance, honey. This is the big time and it better be big."

I watched this discussion take place because I was numb and had taken refuge in a remote corner of my mind. From this vantage point, I had access to many aspects of reality, like the fact that I had no idea who the crowd was. And, an even harsher reality, that the producer had just panned my pitch with just one word and a patronizing smile. Cute. She hadn't even tried to be nice.

Laurie came to my defense. "I told her I wanted to mix in the avant-garde. I want these women to be whatever and whoever they want to be. This show has got to be different than the bodybuilding shows or all this work is for nothing. This isn't just about skin. That's the whole point. This is about much, much more."

The producer turned her over-the-reading-glasses look on Laurie. "Oh, it may be about more, but that's not what your audience is paying to see. Look, you don't have to take my advice, but I'm telling you, I know what I'm talking about. You can't change the course of history with one show, honey. You might be able to over, say, fifty years' time," she said, waving her arm in a wide arc and then pointing her finger and addressing the final comment to me. "But with this crowd, that's only if you show enough skin."

"So, what do you think it needs?" Laurie asked. The three women discussed walls of bodies and quick transitions, but Laurie was insistent about the "theatrical elements," as she liked to call them. I was still digesting the fact that my work had been called "cute" and dismissed without even the slightest consideration. Mr. Kitty was getting annoyed with the animated arm waving, which shook the bed, disturbing his nap, and he jumped off.

The producer threw her hands up in the air, "All right, all right. You've got your vision. Just make it fast and loud. This show has got to be tight."

When Laurie returned from her trek with the producer to the door, she assured me I was on the right track, though I detected the first note of doubt I'd ever heard in her voice. She looked at me distractedly. "You okay?"

"She called it cute."

"I know. I don't think she really gets what we're doing. Let's just work on the finale a bit. If you can make that big and bold then I think we'll be fine." Cecilia concurred. Laurie stared at the photos on the wall. "I've got to get to the gym. Look at me! I haven't been all week!" It was jarring to notice her body again, looking as big and hard and unstoppable as ever. I had become used to it, the same way you get used to a friend's new hair color even though it doesn't look quite right.

Laurie pulled her gym things from a drawer in the dresser in the hallway and launched into a description of what she wanted her performance to be. She wanted to adapt Aeschylus, to write a tale of Magna Mater, and be like a female Phoenix rising from the ashes, complete with a Greek chorus. "How's that sound?" she asked, doing calf raises on the single step between what used to be the bedroom and the living room.

I often wondered later why I didn't say, "What the hell are you talking about, lady? Didn't you hear what she just said? I think that sounds utterly undoable, just like the rest of this ridiculous show." I wondered why I didn't collect my things and thank her for the interesting adventure right then and there. But I didn't. I told her I thought it sounded interesting.

I've concluded that there are three possibilities that could explain my behavior.

One, age. For better or for worse, there's no stopping a twenty-three-year-old with a Big Break.

Two, the question of vision. There's possibility in vision that urges you to surmount the biggest obstacles. Laurie's conviction—the way she believed that all expressions should be represented in the show, the way she didn't back down in the face of Broadway experience—made me believe that she saw something that perhaps I didn't yet see. That maybe there was some alchemical process that would marry these seemingly disparate pieces and magically create something I had never imagined. That Alice Walker and the White Lace Affair might not be as odd a combination as I thought and that this marriage, this embracing of various facets of femaleness could in fact create a new vocabulary. The new female voice.

Which brings me to three, delusion. Laurie has an incredible effect on people. They do what she wants because they believe in what she says, and she appeals to that part in them that wants to effect change and make the world a better place. History shows that most major change is met with opposition. If *The Celebration* was truly unprecedented, I reasoned, then it only made sense that we would encounter naysayers who didn't "get it." Proceeding from this premise, one could believe that the amount of opposition was in direct proportion to the revolutionary quality of the work, thereby turning a rejection of the show into an affirmation of its sheer brilliance.

In other words, I talked myself into it. Instead of saying, "This is insane. I quit," I walked with her to the gym, planning her performance. Laurie would be painted gold like a statue. We would have a fake boulder she would rise up from behind and stairs you couldn't see so that it looked like she was climbing a mountain, striking poses on the way, until she reached the top. As we walked, me so much taller than Laurie, she so much wider than me, Cecilia trailing behind, people often moved out of our way, stopping to stare at her as we passed, creating a thin stream of turned heads in our wake.

9

What It's Like to Wrestle for a Living

Doing sessions" is the expression used to describe the act of wrestling for money. You could ask someone, "Do you do sessions?" or say, "I just did a session with a client." If you're the type of person who asks, "Do you do sessions?" you might also have other questions, like "Why do you do sessions?" or "What happens during a session?" or "How do you book a session?"

One answer to the question of "why" is obvious. Sessions pay well. Very well. About $300 to $350 an hour. It's not unusual for a woman to be flown somewhere for a day or weekend and to be paid anywhere from $1,500 to $15,000 (plus expenses), depending on the type of wrestling they are doing. One wrestler, let's call her Mary, was once flown to Bellevue, Washington, for a day. She had a wrestling session with her client in the morning, they went out to lunch, and they had another session in the afternoon. Afterward the gentleman drove her to her hotel and then picked her up in the morning to take her to the airport. Another time, Mary was offered $5,000 to be flown to Saudi Arabia for a weekend, but she didn't go. She didn't think Saudi Arabia was the best place for a female bodybuilder. Another time, Mary was flown to the Midwest by a dentist who wanted her to walk around in lingerie and flex her muscles so that he could look at her legs, calves, and biceps. He didn't even want to wrestle. He wanted to talk. About nutrition and working out. So they went to lunch and then to the gym, where Mary showed him some training techniques. That was it. "That was pretty lucky, though," she said. "Most guys aren't as much of a gentleman."

Every single kind of man you can imagine books sessions. Mary has never had a woman book a session, although once a man's girlfriend accompanied him and another time a man's dominatrix came along to make sure he wasn't doing anything he wasn't supposed to. For the most part, though, Mary has just wrestled men of all different ages, from eighty-year-olds all the way down to eighteen-year-olds. She has wrestled little nerdy guys, a couple of guys who looked like models, a Hasidic Jew, Japanese guys, African American guys, Arabs, millionaires, and poor guys. One guy lived in a rooming house because he couldn't afford anything else, but he found money to have sessions with her.

There is a term for men who wrestle women: schmoes. Mary doesn't like to use the term and feels it is derogatory, but talk to anyone else in the industry and all you hear about are schmoes. Comments like, "Thank god for the schmoes because if it wasn't for them, [financial support for] female bodybuilding wouldn't exist." Not all men who wrestle women consider themselves schmoes, however. Bill Wick, who could be considered the founding father of session wrestling (though without a definitive history of "session wrestling" it is difficult to discern the exact origins), does not consider himself a schmoe. Wick was married to one of female bodybuilding's greatest competitors, Kay Baxter, back in the early 1980s, when the sport was first gaining ground. Baxter was one of the first women to put on what was then considered bulk and is famous for her beauty and grace, but her life was cut short when she died in a car accident in 1988. Wick and Baxter loved to wrestle. Wick had wrestled in college, coached on the college level, and gone on to coach the first U.S. women's wrestling team in 1989. For Wick, athletics has to do with function rather than aesthetic, so when his wife wanted to learn to wrestle, he was thrilled by the chance to show off her muscles working, not just oiled up and posing onstage. He taught her wrestling moves, and then they got other men to "scrap around" with her, videotaped it, and sold the videos. Wick has been making (and selling) videos ever since. He thinks Baxter was the first woman to wrestle for money, though back then she didn't do it for the cash—she made only $25 a session. She did it to practice her wrestling moves. Wick would even coach the guys, who were in awe of a female who could actually challenge them on a physical level, but usually they couldn't even come close to competing with her. For Wick and Baxter, wrestling was purely an athletic event.

For this reason, Wick does not consider himself a schmoe. He says that the difference between him and schmoes is that schmoes are "little nerdy guys who weigh a hundred thirty pounds, wear glasses, and have nineteen pens in one pocket," for whom "wrestling is a sweaty-palms, exciting, heavy-breathing kind of event." Not so for Wick. For him, he says, it's just fun, like kids playing. He likes the physical contest—even though he knows he can win whenever he wants. When he started he wondered whether strong female bodybuilders could beat him; he found that it was the technique, not the brawn, that wins on the mat.

Back in those days, to book a session you used to have to go up to a muscular woman and ask, "Hey, would you wrestle me? I'll pay you a hundred bucks." Or you'd have to find a way to get your name onto the mailing list of a newsletter that was distributed to a handful of men across the country featuring information about the twenty or so women who were wrestling at the time. It was a subterranean scene.

By the late 1980s small agencies were forming, one of the first of which was Physical Culture in Brooklyn, New York. Founder Robin Parker was a sculptor in the city at the time. Like most artists, she was struggling to find ways to make a living and still have time to make her art. The stock market had crashed and people and galleries were becoming less interested in buying art. She had been lifting weights in her loft and was beginning to get into sculpting her physique. She was also beginning to star in wrestling videos, which required very little time and paid handsomely. One thing led to another, and she began booking private sessions with men who then wanted to meet other women who wrestled. She set up the sessions, offered a facility and a mat, and took a commission. Physical Culture was born. Parker ran the agency for the next six years, developed a long client list, and enjoyed a comfortable life in New York. All of which was a good thing for an athlete training to be in top condition who didn't want to hold a regular job.

With the advent of the Internet, however, booking sessions has become much easier. All you have to do is Google "wrestle muscle women" or "wrestle female bodybuilder," and you'll end up with more than enough options. Among other things, search results will contain personal websites of wrestlers such as Bunny Glamazon, a 6-foot-3-inch, 220-pound wrestler who offers services like "fantasy wrestling," "muscle worship," or "light domination." Search results will also contain websites of referral agencies that have moved their business online and manage a number of female wrestlers. You can browse photos to see whom you might want to wrestle, what her upcoming travel schedule is, and what her specialties are. At ironbelles.com, a website that books close to fifty different women, their "nationally noted muscular beauties" are available for wrestling, muscle worship, fantasy role-playing, light domination, posing, submission, video production, lifts/carries, personalized training, massage, lingerie posing/modeling, oil wrestling, and fantasy/cuddle wrestling. They are in the business of "bringing your muscle fantasies to life," but that's it. They explicitly state that they are not a "full-service" organization.

Mary does only what she calls "light, playful wrestling." Other women advertise all-out, hard, competitive wrestling, but it's not worth it for Mary to get hurt. Instead, she does things like put men in headlocks and tell them to try to get out of it. "Usually they don't even try to get out. They just want to feel what it's like for me to have them in this hold. They just want to feel my arms." Another thing she does is put her clients in head scissors: that's when you put someone's head between your thighs, lock your ankles together, straighten your legs, and then flex your thighs as hard as possible, squeezing the person's head. There are men who love that. They want to see how hard a head scissors they can take. Mary also does body scissors, which is the same thing as head scissors except that you wrap your legs around someone's waist. And then there is the grapevine leg hold, where you interlock your legs with someone else's and then straighten them out (which really hurts); and the full or halfnelson headlock, where you stand behind someone, weave your arms (or one arm, for a halfnelson) under his and then put your hands behind his neck. You can actually break someone's neck if you push down on it too hard.

Competitive wrestling is more like hand-to-hand combat, where the wrestler and the client are trying to take each other down. Some clients want to wrestle hard, but Mary thinks it's too dangerous. She figures that she's stronger than a lot of men, but a medium-sized guy could overpower a woman if he really wanted to. She's seen numerous sessions where the woman wins, but she knows that the men are often playacting. One time, however, it was no act. She was doing a double session with a woman who wrestles rough. The woman knocked the guy out and had to massage his neck to bring him back. "He was into it, though," Mary says.

Bill Wick can attest to the dangers of wrestling. Wick is partial to body scissors and is shocked by the fact that there are people in this world who have never experienced this type of embrace. In between tips that will provide you with an official Bill Wick "B.A. in Scissorology," Wick loves to regale you with tales of various body scissors he's experienced in his life. His favorite story is when his wife broke his ribs during a particularly amorous encounter. "Kay had a scissor hold on me," he said. "She was having a wonderful time, which I take credit for of course. She was having this thrilling orgasm, and she straightened her legs. I looked down at my stomach and I was probably ten inches wide from side to side and I'm thinking, by God, I can't breath, but I didn't want to interrupt her because it took quite a while to get her in the mood, see. So, she's locked out and squeezing the bejesus out of me and I'm seeing spots and thinking, please God, let this end. Pretty soon, I hear *thunk!* And she says, what was that? And I say, I don't know, honey, but I think one of us is hurt." When his doctor, who knew Wick and Baxter from the gym, asked what happened, Wick told him he ran into a doorknob. His doctor rephrased the question to ask what really happened and Wick came clean. "Kay Baxter wrapped her pythonic pillars of passionate persuasion around my massive, thick chest and broke my fuckin' ribs. That's what happened."

The weirdest session Mary has ever done was a trampling session, (that's when you walk all over someone).

First the guy wanted her to parade around in heels. He wanted to see her calves and legs. And then he squatted down on the floor, and as she was parading around, he threw toy soldiers under her feet so she could step on them. He took off his shirt. Tension began to build. Then he wanted to be stepped on—so she stepped on him. And then he asked her if she minded putting on his chest the contents of a bag that he had and then stepping on them. She told him she didn't mind as long as it wasn't something alive; she'd gotten a request to step on live snails before, and she refuses to step on living creatures. "When I opened up the bag, it was a bag full of light bulbs," she recounted. "Christmas light bulbs, all kinds of lights bulbs. He wanted them on his chest, and he wanted me to step on them and pop the light bulbs. He came equipped. He had Bactine and everything. He brushed it all off, there was a little blood, and he was like, 'That was great. That was extreme trampling.'"

Mary didn't find that session super-enjoyable, she wasn't exactly "into" it, but she thinks of herself as pretty open-minded and felt that as long as it wasn't hurting a living animal she could do it. Laughing, she said, "It wasn't like I was hurting anyone except him, and he wanted me to, so I'm like, okay."

Aside from the money, Mary has mixed feelings about wrestling. On the one hand she finds it interesting. She's curious to know what kinds of ideas are in people's minds. "It's a psychological thing," she said. "You're dealing with people's psyches and emotions. The admiration for muscle women is like this emotional thing in a lot of these guys that they have kept bottled up since they were a kid. They are just in awe, and on several occasions they've told me it's from childhood. Something spurred it on, but they remember an image of a strong woman or a particular woman who was athletic or muscular, and that one woman did it to them. Then later, all of the sudden there are women available that will see them and allow them to touch their muscles, and they have things in their heads about what they want to do. Some want to be picked up and carried around or squeezed really hard or held like a baby. They want to feel your power, feel your strength. They want to be overpowered or dominated."

Despite how interesting it can be, Mary also finds the work physically and mentally draining. She comes back from, say, two days of sessions in New York, where she's dealt with twenty different people's minds, and she feels emotional, a little depressed, and tired.

"It's really complicated, to be honest with you. Somebody on the outside might be like, 'Oh, they just want to feel you up,' but to me it isn't really like that. It is more like they are kind of exposing a very deep need to me, and I am fulfilling that need." Many female wrestlers are sensitive to the emotional nature of their work, but there are others who just find it fun or, conversely, find the whole scene ridiculous. One wrestler explained, "I began to ask myself, why do I kill myself so these men can get excited? A lot of these guys have this lame male ego thing and they want to prove that they can win, but if they want to prove that they're some kind of man, why don't they wrestle men, then? None of this is about strength or wrestling, anyway, because a skinny girl can kick your ass if she has good technique. They really just want to be close to your body, so I got more into the worship thing. They like strong women and that is why they are there, so I let them admire me." Another wrestler put it this way: "It's just stupid. But hell, if men are dumb enough to pay me hundreds of dollars just to see my muscles, why not?"

There are a number of old-timers who are getting out of the business altogether. Industry insiders claim that wrestling enjoyed a heyday before the age of the Internet. With the boom of the World Wide Web, however, all kinds of other people have become involved in what previously was an underground scene of muscle worship. Non-bodybuilders, a.k.a. S&M "mistresses," and other women looking for a new way to make money discovered sessions and also began booking clients. The influx of new blood served to broaden the range of services rendered, and this pushed the industry from what purists like Wick considered unadulterated fun to nothing short of prostitution.

"The problem was that you would wrestle with a guy, and he would say, 'You're not being cool because so-and-so did this [sexual act] for me,'" recounted one bodybuilder who quit session work. "And you'd have to say, 'Sorry, but I'm not going to do it. That isn't what this is about.' And he would say, 'Well, I only paid her two hundred dollars, and she did it.' I started getting away from it because women were starting to undercut other women and guys were getting so much more for so much less money and I thought it was getting too freaky, too scary."

Considering the economic downsizing of the sport of women's bodybuilding, however, some still believe wrestling represents a convenient way to make a living while competing. Charles Peeples believes all bodybuilders should take advantage of it. Peeples is a huge fan of female muscle and runs a company called The Valkyries—its tag line is "A Hard Woman Is Good to Find"—that sells T-shirts, posters, and bumper stickers with artistic images of strong women with captions like "No Glutes No Glory" and "To Hell with Physical Correctness." His website says that the images are meant to "symbolize all women who dare to approach [a] physical absolute, rejecting the notion that femininity is compromised by muscularity and might. In their best moments, they show, with dazzling clarity, a majesty of power and beauty whose celebration is long overdue."

Peeples celebrates female bodybuilders every way he can. He runs Vixen Hill Farm, a sixty-five-acre family estate near Valley Forge, Pennsylvania, which he allows photographers and filmmakers whose work advances the cause of female muscle to use for shoots. He has established Team Valkyries, an organization that seeks to instill appreciation of female muscle at an early age by offering financial awards to teams of girls who can do the most push-ups, deep-knee bends, and sit-ups. The Valkyries also provides limited sponsorship opportunities to female bodybuilders and tries to arrange publicity for them. And he writes about the industry, articles such as the one published in *Muscle Elegance* magazine in 1998 entitled "No Apologies" in which he laments the lack of magazine coverage and diminishing prize money for female competitors and proposes wrestling as a viable alternative for women looking to make a living as a bodybuilder.

Who's really celebrating female muscle in anything greater than infant portions? Faced with onslaughts of pneumatic swimsuit cuties, we're lamenting the imminent demise of women's bodybuilding, a keening we've heard since the Dunlap days. But women's bodybuilding isn't dead; it's alive and well—on the Internet. It's outright *booming* on the Web! And that's giving the Powers, the Gate-keepers of bodybuilding all kinds of heartburn.

They can't control this medium, not its content, nor the revenues it generates. Like the Federal government, also seething at cyberspace's challenge to its hegemony, all the Powers (read: IFBB, NPC, and the magazines) can do is pretend to ignore it. But if they were smart, they'd learn from it. And one of the first thing's they'd notice is the Web's unapologetic embracing of female muscle's sensuality.

Of course any suggestion that muscular

women possess sexual allure provokes self-righteous howls from militant feminists and bodybuilding purists alike. The feminists' agenda is a no-brainer, as they attach malevolence to any male interest. The purists are well-intentioned, as they inevitably want female muscle to succeed artistically and athletically, but in some sort of impossible vacuum, devoid of sexual potency.

A fool's errand; even if Freud exaggerated the influence of the sexual urge on everything we do, there's no way we can deny a primal male impulse. That impulse is driven by visual stimuli. That impulse is inexorable. And yes, *that impulse spends money*. So if the competitive arena has failed her, the commercial arena ignored her, and the public arena scorned her, the Physically-Advanced Woman must consider that impulse.

And she has. Fed up with having her gender questioned and her sex appeal denied (even as the swimsuit models have theirs hyped), she's exercising her options. The marketplace is huge, but not discussed in the magazines, whose coverage of female bodybuilding represents only the tip of a titanic iceberg. It's exotic dancing, private posing, domination, and "muscle worship." It's mixed-wrestling, "lift and carry," and those videos you see advertised back on page 256. It's many of the top names in bodybuilding, as well as big names in corporate America. Names and money you wouldn't believe.

Mary makes upwards of $50,000 a year from her website. On it she posts photos of herself for free and has a member area where subscribers have a choice between monthly and yearly subscriptions giving them full access to member-only photos. She's thinking about quitting wrestling entirely and living off the money from her website, since her boyfriend isn't too keen about her doing sessions.

Cheryl Harris brings home well into the six figures from her online empire, which includes ironbelles.com, from which she receives a 20 percent commission for booking sessions and profit from the videos and DVDs she sells; ironbellesvideo.com, which features full-length video-on-demand from seventeen different video production companies; and ironbellesfantasytheater.com, where members can access short video clips.

Harris competed as a bodybuilder until she retired in 1996 because, as she says, the sport broke her heart. She began wrestling and shortly after started ironbelles.com. The number one satisfaction that Harris received from wrestling (which she only does occasionally and only locally now) was financial freedom. Nine years later, Harris works from home in her bare feet and shorts. She has four computers and a video server. She works as much as she wants, when she wants, and still works out to keep herself in shape. If she can offer other women the same freedom, then she feels she's done her job. "I've opened up the market for women to do sessions," she explains. "If I can do that and get some money while I'm at it, at least I'm doing something constructive for them, because competing is not it."

It's unclear just how many women wrestle. Estimates range from 20 to 80 percent of all competitive female bodybuilders—it depends on whom you ask. Mary wasn't sure. After thinking about it for a few minutes, she determined that it was probably a lot. But how many of them do it because they like it and how many do it because they feel they have no other choice, no one can say for sure.

Millie Carter strikes a classic pose.

Paula Suzuki onstage during The Celebration *poses to Janet Jackson's* "Control."

Doughdee Marie hoists her boyfriend over her head: "The man, to me, is a man, and I still want to look up to the man. So I look up to him this way." –Doughdee, half-jokingly explaining why she enjoys hoisting men in the air.

Linda Wood-Hoyte, as Cleopatra, flexes with Marc Antony.

The cast strikes their poses onstage. Centered in front is Nicole Bass, a.k.a. Superwoman.

Colleen Colley sets a national record in her weight class, clean jerking 231 pounds during The Celebration.

(above) Thea Bennington flexes.

(right) Paula Suzuki from behind.

Karla Nelson displays her remarkable muscles onstage.

Laurie Fierstein is hoisted on to the cast's shoulders during the grand finale of The Celebration.

10

The Celebration: Act II, Scene 2

I n the four weeks remaining before the show, female bodybuilders and strength athletes around the world were getting ready for *The Celebration*.

In Montreal, the bodybuilder Colette Guimond was planning her Tigress routine (she admired the strength and grace of felines) and was preparing for her first trip to New York. You could cut her French-Canadian accent with a knife, but you didn't want to because listening to the way she slid between words was almost as satisfying as eating chocolate—though it was hard to understand exactly what she was saying. Colette had just won the Canadian Championships in the lightweight division, but still considered herself a novice. Going to New York was a dream come true—she would get the chance to meet female bodybuilding greats such as Karla Nelson and Nicole Bass. It was the Big Time. Not to mention that there would be a paying audience very into female muscle.

In Saudi Arabia, the African American bodybuilder Millie Carter was living with her husband on an army base when she got word of *The Celebration*. She didn't know what she wanted her performance to be, nor did she care. That could be figured out later. She was just happy to spend an all-expenses-paid weekend in New York in the company of women who understood her proclivity for building muscles.

In Germany, Christa Bauch (a.k.a. the Ice Princess and, incidentally, the mother of three) wanted to come for the show, but she also wanted to compete in the Ms. Olympia competition, which was scheduled for just a few weeks later. She didn't have enough money for two separate trips, so Laurie found someone in New York to put her up in the intervening weeks. That person was Robin Parker, the owner of Physical Culture.

Through Physical Culture, Robin had the capacity to generate all kinds of buzz for the show. Between the women she booked sessions for (like Colette Guimond) and her long client list, she was a veritable hub of connections. After receiving Laurie's phone call, Robin printed news of *The Celebration* in her newsletter, which in turn attracted major financial backing for the show. Ticket sales rose rapidly. With Robin's mellow, Western demeanor, you'd never have guessed that she was the kingpin of a major underground wrestling scene (a fact I did not find out until many years later). She was concocting an Urban Shaman routine to music from the band Dead Can Dance. She wanted to work with the four elements, but I urged her to reconsider the use of fire, due to prohibitive insurance costs.

On Long Island, Linda Wood-Hoyte, the then fifty-year-old corporate executive, longtime bodybuilding judge, and competitor, had been through years of ups and downs in the sport—politically and workout-wise. *The Celebration* took all the angst and turned it into something just plain fun. Linda had big plans to be the first black Cleopatra ever seen onstage. She wanted to be carried in on a litter on the shoulders of very fit men and delivered to Marc Antony, who would join her in a duet posing routine. As far as Linda was concerned, the sky was the limit.

There were still others such as Karla Nelson from Minnesota (Miss America); Thea Bennington from Texas (The Female Godfather); Paula Suzuki from Hawaii (posing to Janet Jackson's "Control"); Tina Lockwood from Southern California (Vampire); and the self-proclaimed largest woman in the world, 6-foot-2-inch, 203-pound Nicole Bass from New York (Superwoman). Bass had once been told that women can't build muscles, which had infuriated her to such a degree that she started bodybuilding just to prove them wrong.

Meanwhile, Laurie was drumming up support for the show, putting in calls to people such as Bill Wick—who initially thought that her idea would not fly. He didn't want to pop her bubble, so instead of saying, "It's not gonna work because there's not a whole lot of people into it," he told her, "Well you never know unless you give it a try." Wick planned to attend.

The industry as a whole was not feeling warm and fuzzy about *The Celebration*. Charles Peeples first learned about it at the Jan Tana Classic bodybuilding competition, when Laurie asked him if she could put flyers on his T-shirt table. He was happy to oblige her and helpfully passed out the brochures, which sported a hypermuscular female torso. When Robert Kennedy, the publisher of *MuscleMag*, walked by, Peeples yelled to him, "Hey Bob, you want one of these?" Kennedy took one look at the image and then looked at Peeples with a look that Peeples describes as "absolute rage" and said, "You actually like that?" You could say that Laurie was experiencing far more success generating excitement for the show outside the bodybuilding industry.

As for me, I was experiencing various levels of success myself. After meeting with the producer, I forged ahead, not looking back. There was no time for second-guessing. Participants had to be contacted (whether they returned my calls or not), details needed to be finalized, and I had actresses to prepare—actresses with little to no experience on the stage. Cecilia's odd lot of friends from her class were like the baseball players in the movie *The Bad News Bears*—big on heart and short on skill. Lezlie, tall and graceful with cocoa skin, had a sexy voice that was perfect for her job as a jazz radio DJ. The equally statuesque and mocha-skinned Montez was an executive secretary whose bio read, "Montez learned how to strengthen her backbone and persevere as a result of adversity. Born and raised in the South Montez's life has been spent trying to keep other's people's feet out of her butt." Cindy was a Chinese American martial arts instructor and personal trainer whose card read, "Let me bring out the best in you." Reserved and shy Rochelle had a complexion as luxurious as dark chocolate pudding. Cecilia's daughter, Bridgett, attended the School of the Performing Arts and was a teenage version of herself, lanky but with the same Orphan Annie–red hair and freckles. And finally there was Starr, a friend of Bridgett's from school who was stocky like an athlete and had an easy smile that reminded you that she was still just a kid.

As with most new actors, they were given to either over- or underacting and few of them had ever been in front of a big crowd before. But they, like me, felt the awesomeness of the opportunity, felt the very real possibility of being discovered, and probably daydreamed, like me, of the day when they would look back at this event and be able to say, "That's when it all began."

They were also given to fits of insecurity, though who could blame them? When, because of the bodybuilders' failure to return my calls, I was unable to plan the show because I didn't know more than a handful of performance themes, which led to my inability to produce a script that the actresses could work with, they at first suffered politely in silence. But it didn't take long before they railed at me at rehearsal. How could they prepare without a script? What was the plan, anyway? What would their roles be? I had no answers for them, so week after week I made up acting exercises to keep them occupied. In retrospect, the exercises were rather esoteric, but in the absence of actual content, I figured I would focus on the concepts behind the show and build these ideas into their psyches with exercises that explored ideas like what it was like to feel big and what it was like to feel small.

It got so bad that one day, Montez threw a fit and, wringing her hands, yelled at me that the whole thing was causing her so much distress she had to increase her therapy to two times a week to manage her excess anxiety. This episode prompted me to wrangle the random performances I did have and adapt something, anything, for the emcee segments in between.

By the week of the show, things were beginning to fall into place. I hired a choreographer to make the Opening and Finale say *"Bam!"* My best friend from college, Dianné Aldrich, a dancer, was the willing candidate. Drums would beat while women wove themselves into a dance that evolved into a human pyramid—an impenetrable wall of female muscle smiling and glistening and very pumped up. All in all, it was tight. It could work. I had schedules, rehearsal halls, and a crew. Tight schedules, but I had everything—organizing the performances, costumes, makeup, music, lights—planned down to the most minute detail. With everyone's cooperation, I knew we could do it. I even had my debut dress—a chocolate brown 1930s-style velvet dress with a deep V-neck and tight waist that my parents bought me because I couldn't afford one on my own. As the playwright and director, I was ready to make *The Celebration* happen.

Whatever my preparation, however, there was nothing that could have readied me for the phenomenon of nature that gathered in the lobby of the Howard Johnson's at Fifty-first Street and Eighth Avenue, on the night of the kickoff meeting. I had commandeered a corner of the hotel foyer marked by colonial accents: faux wood paneling, a branching brass chandelier, beige couches with scroll-type arms, and a carpet patterned with beige, burgundy, and forest green triangles stacked upon each other in repetition. A tall brass podium that was supposed to resemble an elaborate music stand listed the hotel's special guests. "The Celebration of Awesome Female Muscle Display" it said. I had dragged two couches so they were positioned side by side, and had pulled a small table in front of them where Laurie and I would stand to address the group.

Just then a small clan of sassy-looking warrior-like ladies came bounding from the elevators. A second lift dinged and another group emerged in their dolled-up 'dos and gym sweats, jeans and cutoff T-shirts. They clustered in the center of the lobby, and I found myself staring, along with a handful of other hotel guests, at the fantastic specimens.

Clothes were secondary to the spectacle of their bodies and served only to accentuate carefully cultivated body parts. If there was an opportunity for exposure it was taken—short tops showed off washboard abs; deep V-necks revealed ravinelike cleavage; sleeveless shirts exposed fantastic shoulders. The women reminded me of cats in the sun, basking in the glow of attention bestowed upon them by dumbstruck onlookers who didn't even bother to pretend they weren't looking. There was an unspoken agreement: you may look at me because I am something to be looked at and admired. Outsiders sometimes approached one of the women for a picture and were graciously indulged with a flexed bicep and a smile.

One look at the group and you saw people reveling in

being reunited. Some women came alone, but many were accompanied by equally massive boyfriends or husbands. Hugs and squeals characterized each greeting while they tried to remember the last time they had seen each other. "Was it at the Ms. Olympia? Or the Nationals? What did you weigh in at there? Well, you're looking ripped now." A second look, and you saw mythic images of strength. Literally larger than life, they seemed untouchable, powerful in being exceptions to the rule. Yet look again, and you saw the hint of nervous girlishness that lingered in their ever-ready smiles and eyes that quickly scanned each other's bodies; you could have mistaken the scene for a high school bathroom on prom night.

A revolving door from the street threw Laurie into the room, and the mass of lady warriors rumbled across the lobby to greet her. She beamed like a girl at her own birthday party, hugging the participants one by one. No one knew who I was, but I was too thrilled to care. They'd know soon enough that I was the playwright and director. It was my Broadway debut, and that fact could not be eclipsed by anything.

"Are you with the show?" Colleene Colley planted herself next to me. Dressed in a blue sweatsuit with white lines down the arms and legs, she stood 5 feet 2 inches tall and looked more stocky than sculpted. Colleene was there with a chaperone, Jane. It seemed the national team wanted to make sure that their top athlete was representing her country well. After all, she was slated to set a national record at *The Celebration*, and they had to confirm that the lifts were properly executed. From the way Colleene scanned the crowd, however, looking like a kid in a candy shop savoring all those sweet treats parading before her eyes, I could see why she might need a little minding. She was a person who reveled in her desires and had no problem letting everyone around her know what they were. "Someone told me once that I was a male chauvinist, but I can't help myself. I love women too much," she said cracking herself up. "I'm no chauvinist, though. I'm just a southern dyke with loads of chivalry." Colleene stood with the authority of a top athlete in her prime, surveying the world around her as if everything were hers to pluck and enjoy.

Then, as if she didn't measure up, she rolled her eyes and said, "I do not want any of these women asking to see my biceps." She continued, commenting under her breath, "I just know they're are gonna want to know how much I bench-press." She explained that weightlifters are better known for their speed, technique, and lower-body strength than they are for sculpted muscles. "I'll show them other things, but not my biceps." Then she hummed through her lips like she had just eaten a good piece of pie. "Now, who is that?"

The object of her gaze was Doughdee Marie. Doughdee was neither a bodybuilder nor a weightlifter. She was an entertainer, an ice-skating stunt performer among other things. She had done front flips through rings of fire on ice for Disney. Doughdee bounced around the group with her movie-star long blond curly tresses hanging to her waist. Pink curlers were twisted into the ends of her hair. Doughdee's body was thick and curvaceous. She was bubbly and vivacious, and had an unmistakable laugh, like Woody Woodpecker's, only much higher-pitched and broken up by snorts. Rumor had it she was paid to live in a mansion in Los Angeles and perform stunt acts for the mansion's owner. Doughdee was going to battle her boyfriend, Fritz, onstage to Queen's "Who Wants to Live Forever?" Fritz was half her size. Colleene excused herself to make an introduction.

Standing next to Doughdee was Linda Wood-Hoyte who had a calm and solid presence, as if there were nowhere else she'd rather be than inside her own skin. Robin Parker was a stunning mix of long dark-brown hair, green eyes, and a smile that was warmer than the sun. Colette Guimond, with her kitty-cat eyes and perky body, looked just like the feline she planned to become onstage, only with fluffy, curly hair. Dawn Whitham was grinning from ear to ear and had enough energy to light the entire hotel. Karla Nelson was statuesque and shy.

Everyone looked different than I envisioned from speaking to them on the phone; different from what I heard when they shared their individual struggles with me. Despite the pride they took in their personal transformation, you couldn't help but feel a kind of loneliness when they described their muscles as shields or armor; when they either admitted to childhood sexual abuse or noted that most other competitors they knew had been abused and that their muscles had been built as a kind of protection and isolation; when they recounted that the world thought of them as freaks and competitions as freak shows. On that night, however, no loneliness was evident. They were no longer anomalies toiling away alone in the world. Instead, there was a palpable sense of relief and jubilation in being united with others like themselves—and not under the mantle of a competition. Together, they were celebratory victors of their daily small battles with dieting and lifting that weight one more time and wondering if they look like what the judges want and suffering people's stares and remarks about their bodies. Together, these women were a mighty clan.

We just needed a few more of them to arrive so the meeting could get started.

"Kristin, meet Peter." Laurie strutted up with a man who looked as if he'd been stuffed into his suit. He hadn't outgrown his baby fat, even though he stood six feet tall. Laurie explained that Peter was a silent partner in the project and had been responsible for donating a fair amount of cash. He came from Los Angeles, and she called him a producer. His eyes wandered over my shoulder as he shook my hand, and he excused himself quickly. He hadn't gone far before he returned with Doughdee, who was pulling him back in my direction. After a very enthusiastic hello, she told me their idea: "Peter and I think it would be incredible for the show if I hang from the ceiling by my neck and spin. I've done it before. Crowds love it."

I stared at her, thinking, "You must be kidding," but she kept grinning at me and nodding her head "Yes" in anticipation of my being floored by her contribution.

"Wow, Doughdee, that sounds great." I was practicing my best Director's Rejection of Ideas voice. "But, you know, it's just a few days before the show and the plans are set. Besides, we don't have insurance for that kind of thing."

"Oh, don't worry about that. I can take care of it," said Peter.

I stared back in disbelief.

"C'mon, sweetie, no worries. Look, Peter is going to spend the day tomorrow looking for the rigging. It's easy. I won't fall. I promise. It'll be so rad." She nodded her head vigorously again, as if she thought that if she nodded enough times, I would be swayed. Then, before I could say no, she turned on her heels and bounded off.

Peter's eyes followed her. "Peter." I had to get his attention. "We can't have her hanging by her neck."

"I'll look into it," he said and walked away.

"Nice to listen to the director," I thought to myself.

"C'mon, everyone! Let's get started!" Laurie herded the women to the couches to describe the plans for the upcoming days. Only two-thirds of the women were there. I couldn't imagine not showing up for the kickoff meeting. In theater, production week is sacred. So much has to be finalized, and no one would dream of missing a minute of it. The success of the show depends on it.

I looked at the faces lined in front of me. There they were—awesome female muscle makers, bright-eyed and ready to go. Finally having faces—actually, having bodies—attached to names turned *The Celebration* from a heady idea into a spirited force. Now there was meat on the bones of the skeleton of the show, and in just two days it would be a living, breathing phenomenon that hundreds of eyes would feast on. Last I'd heard, ticket sales were around seven hundred and climbing, just over half of the maximum capacity at Roseland.

But better yet for me, my work would be seen. As Laurie described the rehearsal schedule, I envisioned how reporters would want to interview me. They would want to know how I had pulled it off, how I had seamlessly blended the sacred with the profane. I would tell them that I hoped Brecht would be proud. I would act demure and explain that it wasn't really me. I would tell them that Laurie had ignited my imagination and that the women were just diamonds in the rough and my job was just to know where to cut. I might go so far as to say that I wasn't really a director. I was merely a facilitator facilitating the creative process. In the spirit of *The Celebration*, I would cast off the patriarchal term "director." I was just one of the chorus of female voices. And then I would let them take pictures of me that I hoped would be on the front page of, say, the Arts and Leisure section of the *New York Times*.

After the meeting, feeling very director-like, I pulled Laurie aside to inform her of my directorial decision. I could not believe the feel of her arm under my hand.

"Listen, Laurie, I'm worried. I can't have women not showing up. I'm going to have to cut them." It sounded good. My voice was strong. "There is no way for the light and sound guys to know what to do if they aren't here. And Doughdee wants to hang by her neck and spin. Peter insists on helping her. People can't just do whatever they want. They have to listen to me." I was directing. I was in charge.

Laurie turned on me with a glare in her eye I had not yet seen. "I'll see what I can do about Doughdee, but as for the rest, you are not cutting anybody. This is my show. And these women will never get an opportunity to perform like this again. They could be risking their careers to be here. So if I say they're in, they're in."

She snatched her arm from under my hand and turned from me, as I stood speechless, watching her leave, disappearing into the crowd of zealous chattering Amazons.

11

A Sport Can Face Extinction, Too, Part II

T hose who believe that women's bodybuilding is close to extinction point to the dismal lack of press coverage for female competitors as proof of their theory. They posit that the Fitness and Figure divisions are slowly but surely squeezing women's bodybuilding out altogether. Sure enough, there is a direct correlation between the decrease in coverage for female bodybuilders and the increase in coverage for Fitness and

Figure, a shift that occurred in the mid-1990s when the two new divisions took hold.

The media can't get enough of Fitness and Figure competitors. They especially love competitors with pretty faces who are slim-waisted, full-busted, and fat-free, with abs like a finely grouted tile floor. They look great in bikinis on the arm of a huge guy holding a bottle of [put name of any supplement here]; the ad copy reads "Brand X can help you experience unbelievable growth and build a back that attracts attention!" Magazines like *MuscleMag International* feature them on the covers with headlines like "Beautiful Butts: 32-page Glutes Special." True to its word, the special features full-color pages of women in G-strings, or no strings at all. Female bodybuilders used to enjoy similar kinds of exposure, but now they are rarely featured anywhere.

Although, to say female bodybuilders have "enjoyed" exposure might not be exactly accurate. Industry magazines and webzines have had a history of confusing female muscle with sexuality. In the August 2002 issue of the prominent bodybuilding magazine *Muscular Development*, Colette Nelson, the then two-time U.S. champion, was featured in an article entitled "Extreme Sex." The writer wanted to know what her favorite position was and whether anything was "off limits, like her ass." He also confirmed that Colette had a "hot, phat body primed for either pumping up or porking or both." Not all articles have such a provocative slant, but when journalists aren't extolling the virtues of female muscle, they tend to debate its value. One *Muscle and Fitness* article, "Mass or Class?" pondered how big women could get before they lost their cherished femininity.

Bodybuilder Dawn Whitham finds the proliferation of breast and butt features demoralizing. "Those magazines piss me off. Sure the breasts look great, but why do I want to look at that? Those girls don't even look like they work out. Ten years ago when you opened a magazine there was a feature on someone like Bev Francis, but not today."

Over the years, a handful of magazines have done their best to showcase the physically advanced woman, but these didn't last very long. *Women's Physique World*, published for twenty-one years, is the only one that has survived. Behind it stands a devoted triumvirate: the publisher, Bill Jentz; the editor (and IFBB women's historian), Steve Wennerstrom; and the associate editor, John Nafpliotis. These are men for whom muscular female calves are next to godliness. They have poured over two decades of their lives into promoting very muscled ladies. Bill Wick knew the crew back in the 1970s and describes the whole lot of them as counterculture. "We were breaking barriers to say that a woman should be free to be strong, mentally, physically, spiritually, every way she could be. If she wants to lift weights, climb trees, wrestle men, good for her," Wick says. "It was Wennerstrom, me, Nafpliotis, and Jentz encouraging these women to break out of the social confines that men and women have put on them. The way girls and women were treated used to turn my stomach."

Another fan and friend of the *WPW* team, Al Dauber, recalls how the whole group—they're all the same age, mid-fifties—determined that there must have been some weird astrological constellation the year they were born. It is the only plausible explanation for their soft spot for— no, their magnificent obsession with—female muscle.

It all started in the late 1970s with Bill Jentz's newsletter, *Women and Strength Periodical*, which showcased fantastic female physiques—dancers from New York or circus acrobats, gymnasts, divers, and swimmers. Two of his subscribers, Nafpliotis in New Jersey and Wennerstrom in Southern California, began submitting photos to Jentz for inclusion in the newsletter. By 1980, the men began working together to cover the emerging women's bodybuilding scene and went on to launch *Women's Physique World* on newsstands in 1984. Their goal was to present the full range of female physiques in profiles, pictorials, and contest coverage. In the beginning there was no real range except for the extreme that Bev provided. But over the years, the range has become quite expansive, from slender Figure models all the way to the most muscular women in the world. The magazine has a slight bias toward the extreme physique—because nobody else will feature it anymore—and Jentz, Nafpliotis, and Wennerstrom think it deserves to be seen. For this reason they do not shop for advertisers who would try to influence their choice in content—a problem that nearly all magazines encounter. Instead, the publication has survived on subscriptions, though it is no longer on newsstands. In 2001, *Women's Physique World* moved its operation online.

Witnessing the waning support for female bodybuilding is heartbreaking not only to the competitors, but to fans as well. Charles Peeples waxes poetic when he recalls his first Ms. Olympia (the most important pro contest in bodybuilding) in 1990 when it was held at The Beacon in New York City. Women's bodybuilding had punched through the 1980s dispelling all kinds of myths about what a woman's body could do. The sport was edgy and in vogue. That year, The Beacon was packed for pre-judging, which is normally only partially attended. Celebrities like David Lee Roth littered the place. That evening at the finals an unknown named Lenda Murray wiped out the competition. "It was magic," recalls Peeples. "I had never seen such a decisive victory. Everyone said, 'Damn. Where did this girl come from?' When she won, there wasn't a boo in the house. It was a standing ovation. I've never seen anything like it since in bodybuilding." Lenda Murray went on to become a legend, winning seven more Ms. Olympia titles.

Fast-forward to 2001. The Ms. Olympia was held not in New York City but in Las Vegas, at the Mandalay in some kind of exposition hall. Peeples describes the scene. "It was half an hour before the prejudging was supposed to start, and the workers were still setting up. There were guys driving forklifts around, and the stage wasn't ready. The women were huddled by an exit in their sweat suits being shooed out of the way by the forklift drivers. I remember looking at Steve Wennerstrom, sitting onstage. He looked like he wanted to cry, because he could see how this whole thing was disintegrating."

Determining why women's bodybuilding is disinte-

grating is tricky business. Theories abound. John Nafpliotis remembers how the press skewered female competitors right from the start, but back then attributed the
reaction to culture shock. He speculates that the public
would have come to accept female muscle (just look at the
muscular definition on Madonna or the Williams sisters
today) if drugs hadn't come onto the bodybuilding scene.
Nafpliotis complains that male and female competitors
alike have come to look more like lab creations than
human athletes. Add breast implants to the mix, and, for
the women, matters are complicated even further.

Female bodybuilders "have these very untraditional
bodies," Nafpliotis explains, "which normally I think
people would accept, but add to that unusually large
breast implants, and you compound the perception that
bodybuilders are fake and that it is just a freak show. It is
hard to imagine any other female athlete being pressured
to get implants. They look totally out of place, and it
really adds to the negative perception of the women,
rather than the conventional thought that breasts will
heighten their femininity. It makes them look worse
because [breast implants] don't go on a muscular body any
more than they go on a prima ballerina or a gymnast. It
would be laughed off the stage."

One theory is that this cacophonous mix of aesthetic has tipped the scale of public acceptance against female bodybuilders. "The press hates it," declares Bill Wick. "They don't like the deep-voiced, bearded ladies with the big clits. It's that simple. They used to have a beautiful woman represent their product, like Rachel McLish [in the early 1980s], but then Fitness came along with less muscle, but still the beauty. Now Figure comes along and it's pure tits and ass show. Figure competitors are more physically fit than *Playboy* models. The power structure just does not want a big muscle girl to represent their product."

Many observers feel that alleged drug use is behind the International Federation of BodyBuilders' most recent mandate requesting that female competitors decrease their muscularity by 20 percent. Though given the way male competitors are looking these days, why the IFBB only has concerns about the aesthetics and health of the women is anybody's guess. "You'd never see any notice coming down to the men saying they should go back to looking like Frank Zane (three-time Mr. Olympia in the late seventies), although there have been a few articles in magazines that have suggested that," said Nafpliotis. "[The men] look completely freakish."

Pointing to drug use as the primary deterrent to public acceptance of female muscle is a slightly flawed argument, however. First, the world reacted to female muscle the same way back in the 1980s, when there was little to no drug use. It has no tolerance for what it deems extreme. Second, not all athletes use performance-enhancing drugs and it can be difficult to discern who, exactly, is using them. People associated with the sport are reluctant to estimate the percentage of users, but they usually put it at 95 percent of all athletes. Users seem to fall into two categories: those who have misused drugs and wear the side effects like a neon sign, and those who have been careful in their administration and have reaped the benefits without calling attention to themselves.

Wick articulates the difference. "You can't be a Mr. Olympia without taking drugs. You can't be a Ms. Olympia without taking drugs. It's the same in baseball and the Olympics. If you think a Ms. Olympia is pure as the driven snow, my guess is not pure, but she did it right, meaning she probably didn't overdo it and probably had good supervision. Everybody we see who makes it to the top does it right. They don't get the deep voice, and they don't break out. The others, well, they probably get their drugs from Mexico, pump themselves full of it, and they're not going to go anywhere anyway because they didn't have the genetic potential to begin with. You can't make chicken salad out of chicken shit."

If the female bodybuilders who have made it to the top have also managed to "maintain their femininity," then logic would argue that at least they would get some kind of press coverage. But this is not the case. Lenda Murray, an eight-time Ms. Olympia winner and a universally acknowledged knockout, who once received extensive coverage, doesn't even make the pages of industry glossies anymore.

The trend of disintegration is evidenced not only in press coverage but also in the amount of prize money offered at competitions. Actually, it's not that the total amount of prize money has decreased, but that now it is split with Fitness and Figure competitors. Former Canadian IFBB Pro Lisa Bavington figured out the current allotment of monies in her article "Ms. Representation" (published on her website) and outlines the imbalances of competitive bodybuilding. She determined that in 2003, the men received 73 percent of the total $1,474,500 available in prize money (not including Hummers, watches, rings, and cars), and the women had to divide the remaining 27 percent. Of that, Fitness took 12.5 percent, Figure 7.5 percent (not including supplements, clothing, and paid expenses), while Female Bodybuilding got the remaining 7.5 percent (not including water and snacks backstage).

Stats like these were enough to convince Bavington to stop competing. The environment was simply too unsupportive. "It just wasn't worth it for me. You work so hard to get there, and the girls are very divided, there's no recognition, there's no money, there's no respect. I've been an athlete my whole life, and I've never been treated like this. It just wasn't worth it."

So, is women's bodybuilding actually facing extinction or not? Wennerstrom points to the numbers of competitors as proof that women's bodybuilding is doing fine, thank you very much. Wick says that Wennerstrom is unequivocally wrong and says those numbers may be higher at national shows, but local shows are seeing a paltry turn-out and pretty soon Fitness will take over the world. Robin Parker isn't sure. As far as her own career is concerned, she never says never, but she is having a hard time envisioning herself competing again after news of the 20 percent mandate and after coming in sixth at the 2004 Nationals (an IFBB Pro qualifying show) when she showed up in the best shape of her career, which has spanned eighteen years.

On the other hand, Dawn Whitham, who quit competing in the 1990s, is planning to get back into the game. "I'm not doing it for a trophy or a place. I'm doing it just for me. It's who I am. It's what I am. I don't know anything else." She is now a tattoo artist and her entire back, one full arm, and one half arm are covered in ink. She has also upped her implants to 1,200 cc and styled her hair like G.I. Jane. "I am off the charts. I want to totally freak [the judges] out this summer. They're not going to know what the hell to do with me. I love it."

Not knowing another way of life may be one of the factors that helps keep the sport afloat. Lisa Bavington describes how, if they leave competition, women are left with few viable options to support themselves because of the amount of time they've devoted to constant training and dieting. And, at 185 pounds, they feel out of place in an office environment. Having been so wrapped up in the lifestyle, many competitors find that the skills they acquired in the sport are not successfully transferable to the "real world" and after they retire from competition they doubt their ability to succeed in other areas of life.

Whatever the rest of the world says, however, Bill Dobbins maintains that the whole extinction idea is hogwash. He explains it this way. "This is the first era in all of human history in which women have developed hypermuscularity for primarily aesthetic purposes. This concept is so totally revolutionary and culturally dangerous that even the physique federations themselves have grave reservations about the idea. Sure, the sport faces its challenges, but you can't have a revolution if everyone agrees with you in the beginning."

12

The Celebration: Act II, Scene 3

I was in the middle of a little revolution of my own, and I feared it wasn't going so well. After my mini-showdown with Laurie, it felt like battle lines were being drawn and I had become the enemy. In the hotel lobby on the night of the kickoff meeting, before she finally walked away, Laurie turned her mass of body back around and informed me, "By the way, we're running out of money so your hotel room has been cut from the budget. You're going to have to sleep in the production office." Laurie was going to stay at the hotel. Dianné and I would have to shuttle ourselves downtown.

Later that evening, lying upside-down on the couch/bed in the office/bedroom which looked like it had been ransacked and left for dead—Magic Marker–accosted calendars half hung from the walls; papers littered every chair, table, and nook of floor space; and clothes peeked out from dresser drawers as if seeking escape—I stared at my legs and feet sticking straight up toward the ceiling and began to entertain the notion that my fateful phone call could simply have been a random event in a chaotic world. That there was nothing fated about my role in *The Celebration*. At all. It was entirely plausible that I had simply been in the wrong place at the wrong time. If this was true, then the recent weeks of my life were nothing short of absurd. This thought made me laugh uncontrollably.

Dianné had set about trying different hairstyles with her debut outfit. "What? What are you laughing at?" she asked, standing with her hands on her hips in the middle of the tattered room. Since it was entirely possible that I was laughing at my petite, dancerly friend in her black bustier with shiny silver-sequin peace signs over her boobs, huge hair rollers, and a blue facial mask, I didn't know how to answer her. All I could do was laugh harder.

This got her going and the two of us howled and cackled until her mask cracked, making her face look like a parched blue desert. But then she held up my debut dress and urged me to try it on, and I suddenly felt as if I was going to cry. All I could picture was my parents beaming proudly, sitting next to the famous producer and her famous dancing husband in the front row. And then I pictured Doughdee, blond hair twisted with pink curlers, descending from a cloud of smoke and spinning by her neck with Queen's "We are the Champions" blasting through the ballroom. Which made me laugh again. And so it went until we finally passed out from exhaustion.

The city was just beginning its day when I made my way up Broadway to the Roseland Ballroom the next morning. I decided a walk would do me good and wrapped myself up in a wool coat and bulky scarf and slung my bag over my shoulder, stuffed with a clipboard, scripts, and notes. Street vendors were setting up, and the aromas from their goods were claiming their territory in the chaos of Manhattan. Soft pretzels, roasting chestnuts, and hot dogs accompanied me from one block to the next. I started on Twenty-first Street. From the twenties to the beginning of the thirties I reviewed each performance theme in my mind to assure myself that the flow of the show was still working. From the thirties to the forties I ran through the difficult transitions—from the record-setting lift to the White Lace Affair, from the Vampire to Superwoman. From the forties to the fifties, I couldn't think of anything at all. I was in Times Square. I was in the heart of the city, the heart of the world-renowned Theater District, the heart of dreams that are dashed and dreams that come true, and just a day away from my own debut.

My pace and my breath quickened. It was too early yet for dense crowds. The only people on the streets were either those who worked there or those camping out for tickets to shows like David Letterman. Since I wasn't standing in line with the rest of them, it was only clear who I was. I worked there. I was a Broadway director. Though I had to stifle a giddy smile so as not to give away how green I really was.

When I turned the corner on to Fifty-second Street, there was Roseland Ballroom, a grand dame whose dress had slightly faded. The funky red letters on the vertical sign announcing her to the street passersby made me proud. On the marquee for the world to see, it said THE CELEBRATION OF THE MOST AWESOME FEMALE MUSCLE IN THE WORLD. And wouldn't you know it, *My Fair Lady* was playing at the theater right next door.

Stepping into Roseland Ballroom is like stepping back to an era when a night on the town meant getting all dolled up with furs and fancy gowns for dinner and dancing. Remnants of that age still linger like the sweet scent of a glamorous woman who has recently retired from a room. Broad round columns covered in pleated material run like a spine through the center of the smoky blue-green lobby. The ballroom lies just beyond a wall of thick glass doors with huge, circular frosted roses etched into the center of them. Just inside the entrance is a shadow box with faded and stained rose-colored felt with a list of married couples who first met on the dance floor. Among the close to one thousand names are Mr. and Mrs. Ben Bernstein (1928), Mr. and Mrs. Anthony Domanico (1931), Mr. and Mrs. Charles and Anna Zambito (1948), and Mr. and Mrs. Luis Diaz (1987). There is also a glass case filled with the shoes of famous dancers whose toes once graced the ballroom floor. You can almost swear that you hear their punctuated breath as they moved in time with the music.

An incredible patience emanates from the walls. After the ballroom era ended, the theater saw everything from performances by Billie Holiday and the Rolling Stones to tattoo conventions and Versace fashion shows pass through. Thousands of shows rehearsed, opened, and then closed, only to be replaced by the next one. Roseland, looking grand lounging all around you, simply collected the memories and watched to see what you would come up with.

The dance floor lies before the enormous stage and is shaped like a huge dog bone, slender in the middle, widening out to bulbous ends. A brass fence with winding vines and huge roses separates the dance floor from the carpeted area where large tables once accommodated diners and wallflowers. I felt like I was sneaking when I placed my feet on the shiny blond wood. The smell of stale cigarette smoke caught in the back of my throat, but I didn't care. For that day and the day after, I was the director there. Roseland was all mine.

Women began arriving at ten minutes to eight, their voices waking the hall. Reporters were arriving too, setting up backdrops for photos and getting their pencils and pads ready to dish. At eight o'clock I looked at my list and noticed a few women missing, but we had to start. Dianné took a group off to one side to teach them the opening and the day began with her counting, "And one, two, three, four, five, six, seven, eight . . ."

The first black Cleopatra and Marc Antony spent the

morning in the women's lounge practicing the fight between Marc Antony and the jealous lover who kills him at the end of the posing routine. I was grateful for this, because by the time they came to work with me at their scheduled 11 A.M. time slot, I was already running late. Colette's Tigress routine had taken more time than expected because we had to come up with more moves than just slithering in the grass. Tina Lockwood, who had planned on being a vampire, decided she didn't want to be one anymore, and Cynthia James, who hadn't planned on being in the show at all (she had just come to make costumes for the ladies), decided she would be the vampire. All of this took time to sort out—and then we had to work out how Cynthia would get in and out of the coffin while posing and wearing stilettos. It was a good thing that Linda had her and Marc Antony's posing routine down, because organizing the litter carriers and staging the delivery of Cleopatra from the back of the theater encountered complications when we realized that the lighting and sound booth would be occupying a large portion of the main aisle, making it impossible for the litter to pass. We finally had to remove a few of the chairs to make way for the queen.

Hours passed like minutes, and before I knew it I was

downing my sandwich, reviewing the afternoon's plans, and watching the carnival around me. Two actresses, Rochelle and Bridgett, were practicing using a microphone, determining how far away or close they could be without causing distortion. Stagehands were building little satellite stages for the emcee segments, the sound of their hammers echoing throughout the enormous theater. Cindy was practicing her sword routine while reciting her monologue, which would announce Cleopatra's arrival. Dianné was fretting about the Opening and Finale. Female bodybuilders are not known to be graceful movers, and while they were getting the routine down, she was concerned about their looking more like plastic action figures. As we were discussing this, Colleene came up from behind, slid her arm around Dianné's waist, said, "C'mon, honey, let's two-step," and swirled her off across the ballroom floor, the two of them laughing and dancing to music that only they could hear.

At the back of the theater a spotlight and camera were on Doughdee, who was holding Fritz above her head and was spinning in ever-faster circles. She was practicing the new routine she'd created since spinning by her neck had been officially nixed from the show. The reporter finally got a microphone to her between lifts and with the earnestness of a kid describing why Halloween is so great she explained why she was there. "It's for Laurie. It's an idea that a woman I love believes in. It's hard nowadays for women to come up with ideas and dreams and be able to fulfill them. It's an honor to be able to help her start this and be part of something from the beginning." She paused for a moment and then her Woody Woodpecker laugh erupted. "And maybe I'll lose the weight while I'm at it."

The reporter asked her something about why she was lifting men in the air, and she said, "I think because a guy has never been lifted. It's a role reversal. The man, to me, is a man, and I still want to look up to the man. So I look up to him this way." She demonstrated by laughing and lifting her arms high above her head and looking up to where the man would be if she were holding one.

Sid, the stage manager, interrupted my people-watching interlude.

"Hey. Um, Superwoman refuses to come to rehearsal." Sid looked frantic.

"What do you mean, she refuses?" Sid had my full attention.

"She says she has already planned her performance, and she doesn't have time to come to rehearsal." Sid was tall and lanky like a teenage boy, had a close-cropped haircut, and wore Elvis Costello glasses. She tapped her pen rapidly against her clipboard.

My plan for Superwoman was complicated. The Vampire scene before the Superwoman performance was going to be littered with gravestones (foam of course). The stage crew was going to move all the props offstage, and I had planned to have it appear as if one of the crew got stuck under a hefty stone etched with R.I.P. At that exact moment, the Superman theme music would begin, and Superwoman would appear at the back of the hall and leap through the crowd to rescue the crew member. Superwoman had to come to rehearsal. It had to be rehearsed.

"She says she already knows her part." Sid's eyebrows were raised high on her forehead.

"Will you get her on the phone?" I swallowed the last bites of my sandwich.

A few minutes later, Sid gestured for me to come to the pay phone. She handed me the receiver, and I heard Nicole growling on the other end.

"Look, I've just got too much to do. I don't even want to be in this show anyway." Nicole was so loud I had to hold the phone away from my ear. "I'm doing this as a favor to Laurie. And I look fat. I don't want anyone seeing me up there. I'm too soft. I know Laurie says we can look however we want. I just don't have time."

I didn't have time for this either, but kept my cool. "Nicole, you're awesome! If you look like the picture you sent, you look amazing. And besides, your act is the best one in the show! I need you here. It'll only take fifteen minutes. C'mon. I need you."

She reluctantly agreed and showed up half an hour later. I was working with Biker Chic, Hannie Van Aken, when I heard Colleene gasp, "What the hell is that?" Colleene was in the group practicing the Opening and they all stopped to stare.

Standing at the far corner of the theater, 6 feet 2 inches tall, 203 pounds, our Superwoman erupted from tiny white ankle-high cowboy boots, skin-tight, super-short jean cut-offs, and a T-shirt with rolled-up sleeves. Her halo of shoulder-length blond hair looked electrified. She claimed to be the largest female bodybuilder in the world, and she was yelling at the stage manager, "Where's my telephone booth?"

Colleene looked stricken. "What the hell's that man doing here?"

Doughdee ran over to her and grabbed her by the chin, "Look at me!" she demanded. Wide-eyed, Colleene did as she was told. "That is not a man."

Never one to back down, Colleene pressed on: "What do you mean that's not a man?"

"Look at me again." By now they were almost nose-to-nose. "You need to shut the fuck up. That's enough. This is a woman," she hissed and released her grip. Then, as if to soften the blow, Doughdee gave Colleene a big wet kiss on the cheek. Colleene stood stupefied, though now her awe was split between Nicole and Doughdee Marie.

Nicole's voice boomed through the theater as she made her way toward me. "Where's my telephone booth?"

Sid was running ahead of her. "Nicole says she needs a telephone booth. You never told me to make a telephone booth. We don't have enough time to make a telephone booth."

"Nicole! So glad you came. Now what's this business about a telephone booth?" I'm tall, but my neck still strained to look up at her.

"This is ridiculous! No telephone booth! What kind of Superwoman doesn't have a telephone booth?" Her eyes jumped quickly around the theater, never stopping for more than a few seconds on any one thing.

"C'mon, Nicole. We've been through this. The guy is going to get stuck under the gravestone, and you'll run up from the back of the audience to save him. Remember?

You won't have time to be undressing in a telephone booth. You agreed to this before."

"If there's no telephone booth, then there's no Superwoman." She stormed away to a group of women whom she hugged and began to chat with, as if nothing had happened. The stage manager looked stunned. Then Nicole stomped over to Laurie, and they conferenced for a few minutes. Laurie then made her way over to me.

"Nicole would really like to have a telephone booth. She feels she can't be Superwoman if she doesn't have one." She had a casual tone and straight face as if her request were perfectly reasonable.

"Laurie. I cannot get Nicole a telephone booth in twenty-four hours. It is an impossibility. Just like it's impossible to have Doughdee spinning from her neck. The same way it is impossible to pull off this show of yours if the women don't show up!" I enunciated every syllable and my voice grew louder, like I was speaking to someone who was deaf.

"Can't you just make one out of cardboard or something?" She made it sound like an innocent question.

"Cardboard? You want cardboard in your show? Okay. You got it." I yelled to no one in particular. "Cardboard it is. Make a friggin' cardboard telephone booth for Superwoman!"

Laurie thanked me. "I know this is a lot. It just means so much to me to have these women participate. You're helping change lives. Believe me. Whatever it takes, we'll do, okay?" She reached her hand out to touch my arm. "And listen, don't take Nicole too seriously. She has terrible mood swings. She just flips out sometimes. You just have to calm her down. She'll do the show, don't worry. I just need you to apologize to her."

Before I could respond, Nicole was towering over us. I looked at the two of them, down at Laurie standing 5 feet tall, and up at Nicole standing 6 feet 2 inches, both relentlessly bursting with muscles.

"Oh, I'm just nuts," she said. "I'm crazy. Don't let me freak you out. It'll be just so much better with a telephone booth, don't you think?"

Laurie eyed me, urging me to say something. "Kristin is sorry for not having the telephone booth ready, aren't you, Kristin?"

I couldn't believe that I was about to apologize. But in the name of getting on with the show, I did.

Nicole held out her huge arms for a conciliatory hug, which I accepted. She yanked me into her wall of chest, saying "You know what? This is gonna be one hell of a show!"

13

What It's Like to Take Steroids

C olleene Colley says that she loves steroids so much that she plans to take a cycle of them every year, or at least every other year, until the day she dies. Taking steroids, most notably testosterone, does three things to Colleene that she does not want to live without: increases her sex drive; emboldens her temperament, which makes her feel superior; and accelerates the results of her training. She attributes her overall vitality and lack of petty ailments—such as colds—to the drugs. For Colleene, steroids are nothing less than the fountain of youth and she'll do her best to talk you into taking them, too.

In moderation, of course. As with everything else in life, there can be too much of a good thing. "It's addicting. It may not be physically addicting, but it sure is mentally," she explained. "With steroids, if you work your ass off and cut back on a little fat, you're gonna look great. It gives you an edge you don't have otherwise. So women take more. But more is not better. These women get ugly, but they don't realize how damn ugly they are because they're loaded up and feel confident. They walk around half-naked, but their faces would stop an eight-day clock."

This hasn't happened to Colleene yet. Her face has maintained its delicate detail, most notably a wide and gently sloped forehead, a jaw perfectly proportioned for her head, and a mane of shiny dark brown hair. These are some of the first things to go when the drugs are used incorrectly. Physical side effects usually start with bad acne and can quickly lead to a (permanently) protruding and broadened forehead, receding hairline, baldness, increased body hair, enlarged hands, an enlarged clitoris, and kidney, liver, and heart damage. Emotional side effects include mood swings, anger flare-ups, and the intense need to assert oneself at all times. The fact that

Colleene's voice has gotten so deep that she now sounds like Tom Cruise isn't because she's taken too much, she assured me. It's just that when she started taking steroids back in the early 1980s, she got bad information about the drug she was taking. She was told it was a good steroid for women—but that ended up not being true.

Testosterone works by entering muscle cells and stimulating the production of proteins, which build muscle. But it is also responsible for the development of male secondary sexual characteristics, the ones that kick in when a boy hits puberty. If you take testosterone, you can't have the desired effects without the undesirable ones. Women naturally produce about 5 percent of the amount of testosterone that men produce. So when a woman adds a significant amount to her system, in effect she's adding a dose of masculinity.

Ironically, when a man takes too much testosterone his system responds as though there were an overproduction and the brain limits production by shrinking the testes. A percentage of the excess testosterone is converted to female sex hormones such as estradiol or estrogen, which results in the development of breast tissue. To counteract this, some men also inject themselves with human chorionic gonadotropin, or hCG, a hormone that is produced in pregnant women to help the embryo survive in the uterus. In a male body this hormone helps the testes continue with the natural production of testosterone rather than shutting down.

This quagmire of secondary sexuality confusion and extreme health risk is exacerbated by the fact that steroid use without a prescription is a federal offense—and therefore proper medical supervision is almost always nonexistent. Drugs are bought on the black market for anywhere from $700 to $2,000 for a six-to-eight-week cycle with no guarantee about the quality of the substance. Educating yourself about how to use them can be extremely difficult. As a result, many bodybuilders take too much too soon, too much for too long, come off them too fast, or take the wrong balance of drugs altogether. Many athletes take diuretics to counteract the water retention that often accompanies steroid use. Diuretics increase urine output and are considered useful for quickly losing water weight, but they can make things really complicated, as they are also very difficult to control and can interfere with kidney functioning, which can lead to low blood pressure, nausea, and ultimately heart failure.

Steroids are not the only drugs taken by bodybuilders (and, naturally, bodybuilders are not the only competitors to abuse these kinds of drugs—the problem has spread to nearly all sports). Growth hormone is a popular choice because users can experience a boost in their bulk-up potential but sidestep the bad side effects of steroids. Colleene can spot growth-hormone users a mile away because the drug promotes bone growth in facial bones, and users' jaws and foreheads look as though they're on their way to becoming exaggerated. A newer drug phenomenon involves the use of insulin, which drives the body's water and glycogen into the muscles. This method is desirable because it creates big, rock-hard muscles but doesn't dehydrate you. All you have to worry about is low glucose levels in your blood, because if you let it drop too low, you can go into a coma.

Bodybuilders tend to rely on each other's experiences, both good and bad, to guide themselves through the drug-taking process. Colleene has become something of a "go-to" girl because she's been around bodybuilding and weightlifting since the early days and has been experimenting with steroids since she first began. She can help users determine how much of what drug should be taken and how to administer them, whether as a pill or an injection. For a while, she fantasized about writing a book on the effects of steroids on men and women. She's been watching how each sex reacts to the drugs and has some definite ideas on the topic.

Colleene is convinced that hormones are the key to life and the only thing that separates men from women. "I know what it feels like for a man to feel like he has to fix things, to be in control. When I'm loaded up, my manners are not like they usually are. I feel like I have to take care of who I'm with, but it's more of an aggressive taking care of, not a nurturing taking care of. When testosterone is running through my system, I have a much shorter fuse. I feel superior. Period. And I'm horny as hell.

"Women are usually so guilt-ridden and worried about fairness, and society tries to write that off as being weaker. We aren't weaker. We're just negotiating our emotions better. Whereas on testosterone you're not dealing with emotions so much. You're just taking action."

Colleene has had male bodybuilders come to her after coming down from too much testosterone but before their bodies have begun making it again. It sometimes takes a little while before the flow of normalcy picks up. "I would have men in my office wailing, sensitive, not knowing what was wrong, feeling like they were inferior. It was depressing. They had no clue what was going on. Nine times out of ten they had come off the drugs too fast and their own testosterone hadn't come up to the right level yet, so they were filled with estrogen. They couldn't take it. I'd tell them, 'Girlfriend, that's what it feels like to be a woman.' One friend told me that there was no way in hell he could go through that every month to have a period."

Colleene started taking steroids because she felt she didn't have a choice. She didn't do sports for fun. She did them to win, and when she came up against a girl at a weightlifting meet, she took one look at the competition and knew there was something different. "What is that?" she asked her coach. The girl was thicker and bulkier, and Colleene couldn't tell if she was a guy or a girl. "That is steroids," her coach replied. And the girl won. "There was no way I could have beat her. She was just that much stronger and that much faster. And I'll tell you what; no one could have been training harder than I was. That's when I said, 'Where are the drugs? Give me the drugs. I can't work this hard only to lose.'"

Some competitors have the opposite reaction. Bill Wick recalls when Rachel McLish quit competitive bodybuilding because of drugs. She told him, "I am not taking drugs, and these girls are on them. You can't get that way without them." Cheryl Harris, owner of iron-belles.com, also quit the sport in part because of drugs.

When she made the Top 15 at the Nationals, she took one look at the women's faces who had ranked higher than her and noticed "their jaws, their foreheads—they were turning into something that was a cross between a man and a woman, and I got so scared I said, 'I am not going to compete again, I don't want to look like this.'"

From estimates I've been given by competitors, 95 percent of female bodybuilders use some form of chemical enhancement, for the very same reason as Colleene, but only about 2 percent will admit to it. Stigma is part of it, but mostly the reason they deny it, even though their voices sound deep, dry, and brittle, their skin is thick as leather, and their jaws are wider than any other part of their head, is because they can't stand the fact that people think the physique they're sporting was created entirely by chemicals. "People simply won't accept that women can create a muscular physique by dieting and lifting weight," Colleene explained. "But we can. Steroids account for only about a five percent increase in my size and hardness. The other ninety-five percent is genetics and pure sweat."

14

The Celebration: Act II, Scene 4

O n the eve of the show there were just two more rehearsals left, Laurie's Magna Mater and the Finale.

Laurie arrived at hers looking haggard. "We're almost there," I offered as she shuffled by. There had been too much to do to remain mad about the Superwoman snafu and by the time Laurie's rehearsal rolled around it was all about the business of getting *The Celebration* ready for the crowd—over a thousand tickets had by now been sold.

She walked right in front of me, right under my nose, and I was struck by how short she was. The top of her head only came up to my collarbone. She dumped her heavy bags on the wooden floor of the small rehearsal studio and crawled up on a prop rock and sat hunched over, her face sullen, and watched, as I worked to get the actresses to function as a chorus. We were having trouble. Speaking in unison was proving difficult.

Dianné dragged Laurie from her perch and tried working with her to choreograph the rise of Magna Mater. Laurie's movements were slow, and she was having difficulty remembering the sequence. I thought having verbal cues might help and made the mistake of trying to coordinate the chorus's text with her gestures. We were in the middle of her rise from the Phoenix-like ashes when she yelled, "Stop! Stop this! This isn't going right. I don't know what you're trying to do to me, but it's going to stop now!"

She stood atop her rock and glared down at me, shoulders broad with anger. We all stood slightly amazed. I didn't know what she was talking about.

"Do you know what you're doing to us?" she raged. "Do you have any idea what we go through every day to do what we do? I won't have you making fools of us up onstage. I just won't."

Cecilia looked questioningly from Rochelle to Montez to Bridgett to me. We all returned her expression.

"This chorus is a nightmare. I'm going to be a laughingstock! I have put everything into this, everything." She started crying uncontrollably on her rock. She didn't even try to bow her head or hide her face in her hand. She just stood, arms hanging at her sides, chest convulsing with sobs, facing all of us with tears streaming down her face.

I'd experienced pre-show jitters many times. It can be a horrible affliction. Emotions are running high. Doubt and despair can descend in the blink of an eye, and suddenly you are sure everything you've been working hard for is ridiculous—the worst thing ever conceived of by a human being. It can be debilitating—except, as they say, the show must go on. A mini-breakdown at this point is actually a good thing—cry, get it out, get your friends to console you and tell you how great everything is going to turn out. In most cases, it does. It is not the time, as instinct urges, to change everything. It is the time to stay on course.

I had expected this from Laurie. Despite how I felt about many of her choices, I had to give her credit: she had single-handedly created an enormous event. Producing the show, coordinating the PR, talking her friends into participating—she had done everything. With her apartment serving as the production office, she'd had no privacy for months. I'd been secretly wondering when she would break down. I'd prepared myself for it. I was going to remind her that not only was she producing what had turned into a major Broadway event, but she was swimming against the tide, taking a stand, challenging major assumptions etched in time. Changing norms causes stress, I would tell her. And so does producing shows, especially the ones you're in. I knew the combination could be lethal. But my reminder would be soothing and evenhanded and ultimately would turn her tears to a reluctant smile, and we'd all laugh and finish getting ready for the show.

But it didn't work out that way.

"Look at me! I'm soft! It's humiliating. I haven't been to the gym all week. And I have to get up there with this body. And this piece is not even close to being ready." Her frustration was not diminishing.

I let her rant.

"And the Finale! It's just not going to work! We can't dance. We'll look ridiculous! People already laugh at us on the street! You don't know . . ." Her voice trailed off behind her tears.

Laurie's massive body sagged like a deflated balloon, but her face remained defiant. In that moment she changed from an intellectual physique artist to a muscular schoolgirl who, although she was tough, just didn't want to be made fun of anymore. In that moment it was clear that the whole show was fueled by her need to protect this vulnerability. Her tears told me that, whatever the rhetoric, she was terrified.

It was time to step in. "Laurie, it's the night before the show. It's normal to be worried and even hate everything at the last minute. Now, we've gone over the whole show from beginning to end many, many times. You've loved every piece of it."

"Well, the Finale is awful! And the women hate it! We need more celebration." She wiped her nose with the back of her hand.

"I know. I know you're worried, but remember the producer said that we needed big and bold. We decided this. And I've got twenty-five women to organize, seven of whom I still have yet to see, and I simply can't change things now. We'll polish the Finale in rehearsal tonight. I promise. You have to trust me. You think you don't like things now, you're really not going to like it if we change it."

We stood staring at each other. Our time was up in the

rehearsal space. The actresses were quietly gathering their things and tiptoeing out of the studio.

Laurie pressed on. "I'm cutting the end."

Everyone stopped what they were doing.

"You're what?" I asked. It was official: she had completely lost it.

She sniffed back her tears, a new determination on her face. "We just have to celebrate. Doughdee has a great idea. Everyone will just lift me up on their shoulders at the end and everyone will celebrate. You can't have all these women up there dancing. They'll be the laughingstock."

There was one hour until the Finale rehearsal. We were so close. It was almost over. There was no way I could coordinate these women to "celebrate." What the hell did "celebrate" mean anyway? Did she want horn blowers and pointy hats?

"You don't know what you're saying," I warned.

We were now engaged in the infamous battle of wills—the producer versus the director. Only I couldn't storm off the set in a power move, leaving everyone to scramble in my wake. I had no cachet. No one was going to beg me to return, worried that the absence of my name associated with the show would bring ticket sales down. This was her show, and if she wanted cardboard props, gaps in the line-up, and unrehearsed chaos, I was finding out that I couldn't do a damned thing about it. My only recourse was to make my voice as icy as possible.

"If you change things now," I said, slowly, to make sure she heard every word, "I'm warning you, your show will be one. Huge. Disaster." That was it. The slippery slope had just been slicked, and there was no way I would ever reach the top again. It was a long way down, and that was where my Broadway debut was heading. Down, down, down.

"Think about what I'm saying to you," Laurie returned as icily. "We'll talk at rehearsal in one hour." She grabbed her bag and left.

In Manhattan, it's hard to know where to go when your world is falling apart. If I hadn't had to leave because the rehearsal space was booked for the next hour, I probably would have sat down and drooled, speechless and too exhausted to close my mouth. Instead, Dianné and I went to the Ling Garden Chinese restaurant next door. We sat trying to decide on our next move, asking each other, "Did she just do that?" "What just happened?" With no appetite, we asked only for a bowl of fortune cookies and cracked our way through lame prophesies.

"Where is serendipity when you really need it?" I grunted, breaking the last cookie against the table. Crumbs and useless paper strips before me, I realized a few things. I had one hour to quit. I had one hour to call the famous producer and ask her what I should do. I had one hour until I could tell Doughdee to take her rigging and hang herself with it. Better yet, celebrate with it. Truth was, I had no idea what to do. One thing I did know, however— changing the ending was the worst thing to do.

When we arrived at the Finale rehearsal at the small gymnasium we'd rented for the evening, all the women were there and ready to go. Excitement danced in the air like falling snow, covering everyone with bubbly anticipation. Everyone that is, except the producers.

Laurie and Peter stood outside waiting for Dianné and me. With hushed tones and serious faces, they ushered us into a small room. Under fluorescent lights, Doughdee and her boyfriend, Fritz, sat in two of the six chairs that had been arranged in a circle. Something about the quiet made me feel like a kid at a church service, and all I wanted to do was laugh. I was fighting to hold it back when Laurie nervously announced the executive decision. The Finale would change to a celebration. Doughdee explained the new plan.

"We'll all be out onstage, and then Laurie will come out. We'll lift her up, and everyone will cheer. Ya know, like *Saturday Night Live*." Doughdee's blond hair looked light green under the lights.

"*Saturday Night Live?*" I sneered. Great. Alice Walker, white lace thongs, and *SNL*.

I clearly wasn't getting it, so sunny-Southern-California Fritz patiently explained, "Ya know, how at the end, they all just cheer, dude? They're celebrating."

"That's how I want my show to be," Laurie finalized.

The Celebration was now a runaway train that collided with the proverbial snowball, and the whole tangled, rolling mess was heading somewhere, and all because I dialed the wrong number and reached Laurie on the pay phone in her gym. It felt as if Fate had planted me directly in its path. All I could do was watch.

Someone knocked on the door to see when we were going to start rehearsal. With tears in her eyes, Dianné began discussing how to organize everyone for the new ending. I sat staring at each of the talking faces, picturing myself throwing a tantrum, throwing chairs, calling them names, and reminding Laurie about her vision for artfully celebrating true strength. Sitting on a bunch of female bodybuilders' shoulders was not exactly avant-garde. The group was busy planning, when I surprised myself by interrupting.

"Everything you wanted this show to stand for is finally squashed with this single act!" I had nothing to lose. "As a professional, it is my duty, if you won't let me do my job, to let you know, for the record, that this is the most unprofessional, poor decision you could make. But since I am a professional, I will show a face of solidarity and will go out there to rehearsal and act as if I agree with this very, very poor decision." The group sat staring at me. They were listening, but I didn't know what else to say. Finally I blurted, "I mean, what the hell are we creating here?" Everyone sat silently, waiting for me to finish. I stared back. When I didn't continue, they finished their planning and went out to rehearsal.

The actresses' and bodybuilders' laughs and chatter bounced off the walls like at a high school basketball game. I stepped onto the bleachers and yelled for everyone's attention. I kept my word and, showing solidarity, said, "Laurie is going to show you all how to celebrate. Listen to Laurie now. We're not going to make you dance and build a wall of bodies. You are now going to celebrate." I then sat down and watched.

The actresses were shocked and, noting my air of resignation, threw looks in my direction inquiring what they should do. When I did not respond, they gathered themselves together and set about rehearsing their part of the Finale dance with the zest of sailors on a sinking ship desperately trying to scoop water from the vessel even as it comes pouring in. From the precision and unity of their movements, they appeared to be willing the show to success if only by ensuring that their little bit was as perfect as they could possibly make it.

Tiny Dianné wiped the tears from her eyes, waded into the sea of female muscle, and began teaching them how to lift Laurie to their shoulders. They almost dropped her a number of times, but when I finally left, everyone seemed to be getting the hang of the new ending, and Laurie sat high on the women's shoulders, laughing and shaking her fists in the air.

15

What a Competition Is Like

C rowds gather at bodybuilding competitions for the same reason that crowds gather at any other kind of event where something unique is on display: to view fine specimens that have been cultivated to rarefied levels. At the National Physique Committee (NPC) Nationals in Miami in 2003, competitors could just as easily have been a fine porcelain dish at an antique auction or a cat in a cat show or a horse at the track. The crowd exhibited the same zeal for competition, obsession with sporting details, and passion for judging fairness. But instead of shiny, fluffy coats on cats with a refined skeletal structure or one-of-a-kind pieces of old china from a special collection with only a few remaining pieces in the world, bodybuilding fans happen to think perfectly proportioned bodies with exquisitely large and delineated muscles are next to godliness. Many fans reminded me that physique worship goes all the way back to the Greeks. These fans were especially pleased that women have become part of this ancient tradition.

The prejudging part of the competition happens early in the day and audience members include die-hard fans, friends, and families of the competitors, and other competitors who either competed earlier or will do so later. The auditorium is only partly filled, but from the loudness of the cheering you'd expect it was fully packed. Except for a "Yeah, Sheila!!" you might wonder what there is to cheer about, considering that all the work has already been done before the show and competitors simply stand onstage in front of the judges. Wild yelling in support of favorite bodies (competitors have numbers on their bikini bottoms) accounts for most of the racket, but supporters let rip with tips like "Number eighteen, don't forget to breath!" or "Twenty-two, slow down with your poses! This isn't a race!" With everyone throwing their voice into the din, it smacks of a religious revival where the whole congregation is testifying. They say the damnedest things, like "Mmm, mmm. Look at that girl on the left! Man I could pluck those hamstrings like a gui-tar." "Where's the ass on the girl in peach?" "What are those boobs? Torpedoes? If she doesn't watch it she's going to fall right over!" Everyone has something to say about each and every part of each and every competitor's body—nice abs, great proportion, carrying too much water, rock-hard, what a back, her fake tan looks pink. Nothing passes without scrutiny.

Simultaneously, all kinds of other conversations are happening, like the one that took place between the Figure competitors sitting next to me. One said to the other, "I like your boobs. They're cute. I don't have boobs. I've gotta get some. I'm gonna get some after Thanksgiving, I think. But not big ones, though. Just little half oranges." This was the same woman who later explained to me that a boob job was necessary if she wanted to attract a sponsor. "I mean who would pay someone just to be themselves?" she wondered.

The other topic of discussion heard rumbling around concerns the supposed sex of a handful of people in the crowd. Hands down, each and every person in question had long blond hair extensions, platform heels, and wore some kind of super-tight, super-revealing outfit that displayed mounds of muscle. Breasts are the only variable—some have them, some don't. When one of these people walks peacocklike from a doorway to a seat, eyes and whispers follow them. Once seated, a large circle of heads around them repeatedly sneak looks in their direction, trying to decipher who or what they are.

In the lobby of the theater, salespeople are hawking their wares. You can buy everything from Phat Muscle Urban Gym and Streetwear to ANSI Mega Protein Bars to ProTan products like their Dual Phase Self Action Rehydrating Tan Accelerator or their Instant Competition Color with brush. Tables are packed together and barely clothed models perkily pass out samples of whatever they might be selling. A few bodybuilders who have embarked on their own marketing of personal training videos or calendars also have tables. It seems as if more people are hanging out in the lobby than are watching the show. They're catching up with old friends, perusing the goods, or looking around to see who is looking at them.

You can see competitors close up as they pass through on their way to backstage. Seeing bodybuilders on the day of competition is like seeing wax-museum figures that have come to life. They don't look real. Their hair is done up like a debutante's. Their faces have no fat in them so skin looks more like oddly colored sheaths stretched over their skulls, sucked deeply into eye and cheek sockets. They look more stained and lacquered than tanned, most of them having had their entire bodies painted from head to toe with a product like ProTan's Instant Competition Color. It makes them look better under the lights. Their gaze is a million miles away. Their muscular bodies appear to be the only things bursting with life. Looking almost trapped inside the package of their skin, every muscle seems intent on making itself seen.

In the lobby you can also eavesdrop on the dramas that are unfolding. Some are silly, like who said what to whom backstage or who ignored someone else entirely. Other dramas are more tragic, like the competitor who desperately complained to her friend about a judge who told her right after she came offstage that she might be able to win one day if she got breast implants. Or the other drama that ensued between a competitor's friends and her trainers over who was responsible for not cutting her water intake when she started loading her carbs (the result was that she looked "soft" from holding water). One friend walked away from the quiet argument blaming the trainer for mismanaging the competitor's diet. The friend shook her head and said, "Hell, she's one day off. She peaked yesterday. She's devoted months of her life to this and she's not going to win. It's such a goddamn cruel sport."

The five competitors who make it to the finals held that evening can't just sit around and watch TV all day waiting for the competition. Their preparation turns into an exact science, as they attempt to make their bodies so finely calibrated that judges will award them first prize. If they were holding too much water, they might be able to make themselves harder by eating carbs, like lots of pizza, or holding poses for longer than they can bear, to make a specific muscle more prominent. Or, if they managed to peak at the morning show, then they have to carefully monitor every bite of food and sip of fluid that enters their bodies so as not to disturb their award-winning stasis. And they have to check their tans. They can get blotchy from sweating, so at some point during the day, they may find themselves naked in the kitchen of their suite, arms and legs spread wide to allow someone to take a sponge to every inch of their bodies with tan-colored stain.

For the other competitors who don't make the top five, their days are usually spent with friends and family eating and nursing deep wells of disappointment. Or they are at photo shoots. The pool overlooking the sea at the host hotel in Miami looked like a film set for an action movie. Women in all kinds of get-ups, from bathing suits and bare feet to barely-there dresses and platform heels, held warrioresque poses—one rock-hard arm bent, the other straight and both pointed at the sky, a toe pointed to the side to accentuate lean strips of leg muscle—while photographers snapped away. It was a sight to behold: colorful, moving, momentarily smiling human statues dotting a wide horizon against a backdrop of the raging sea. Between the sound of the ocean and the seagulls and the photographers' cameras, you could hear the question, "Why didn't the judges pick me?" travel across the scene like an echo.

In the evening, after the finals, which is much like the afternoon prejudging event except that it is sold out and everyone is dressed up and glamorous, people go out to eat and party and recount the day's events. The bodybuilder I was with ordered yogurt with a fresh fruit bowl, margaritas, chicken quesadillas, baked brie, pizza, and a salad. Other diners from the restaurant interrupted her dinner to ask for a photo. She obliged, mouth full, stopping chewing only to smile, and then went right back to eating. Friends and fans sit around recounting the show bit by bit over beer, ruminating on the inequities of judging women's bodies. The guys from *Women's Physique World* told me they've been doing this for twenty-five years, as if trying to solve an ancient koan.

16

The Celebration: Act III

Had I been to a competition, I might have known better what to expect at *The Celebration*. I might have been prepared to see loads of people, including the bodybuilders, hanging out in the lobby during the show. Or hear audience members yelling and hooting as loud as they could. Had I put two and two together, I would have realized that when almost every bodybuilder told me she didn't like team sports, what she meant was she preferred to do her own thing; then, I might not have gotten so upset when the women failed to appear on cue or even appear at all. Or, had I known what a session was, I might have understood that their absence at rehearsal was due to a lucrative work opportunity and not a lack of interest in their performance. If I'd had any idea how big the world of wrestling actually was, I wouldn't have stood paralyzed in the middle of the ballroom before the show, looking around at the predominantly male sellout crowd of about two thousand (there is a disagreement on exact numbers—estimates range from thirteen hundred to twenty-three hundred), including, incidentally, my parents, my college theater professors (one of whom had been an esteemed theater critic for the *Village Voice*), a handful of curious friends, the famous Broadway producer, and her famous dancing husband. Had I had the wherewithal to accept that the voice of experience often knows what it is talking about, I might have listened to the producer and at the very least cut the seed-pod comedienne sequence from the show.

But I didn't.

I watched the dress rehearsal, which was supposed to end at 5 P.M., run until 7:30, half an hour after the doors were supposed to open to the waiting audience. With an endless flow of forgotten lines, botched cues, performer no-shows, and missing music, I considered my fate sealed.

So I left. Right in the middle of rehearsal. Dianné and I had left our bags at the production office that morning, figuring we'd sail through the day and have time to go back and get dressed before the show. I don't know why we thought things would go as planned. So when the stage manager quit at five o'clock, that seemed as good a time as any to get our things. I figured *The Celebration* was going on with or without me—and in my haze of resignation I'd become oddly obsessed with wearing my debut dress. Funny what becomes important when nothing else makes sense. Feeling absurd and giddy, like I was running away from home, I made my way downtown in a cab. I grabbed my dress and Dianné's peace-sign boob top, turned around, and went right back to Roseland, wishing that the terrible traffic on the West Side Highway would swallow me whole.

I returned to find throngs of men outside the ballroom trying to buy tickets on the street. I pushed my way through the crowd, only to be blocked by the bouncer, who didn't believe who I was. "I'm the frigging director!" I barked. He rolled his eyes as if to say, "Sure you are," and left me waiting outside while he checked on my status. An endless sea of slightly balding, slightly paunchy, kind of pasty men surrounded me. Schmoes. I didn't know who they were at the time, but they struck me as remarkably generic. There was certainly a handful of New York artist types mixed in, but these paunchy men were the primary audience for *The Celebration of the Most Awesome Female Muscle in the World*. I felt nauseated realizing that the producer was right. They certainly weren't there for "art."

The doors finally opened, and I moved with the mass oozing into the ballroom like lava.

The lobby filled with the adoring fans, some with awestruck faces like children seeing their first Disney character in real life. They swarmed the tables where bodybuilders had built mini-shrines to themselves laden with T-shirts, mugs, and videos. They lingered, waiting for the chance to get an autograph or to have a picture taken with their favorite bodybuilder, perhaps in a head-lock. I wandered around, aimlessly at first, not believing what I was seeing, until I entered the ballroom. There I noticed my family, my father looking confidently toward the stage as if his determination would make the show a success, my mother suspiciously eyeing the man sitting next to her, and my older sister looking around bewildered. Then, one of my professors appeared in front of me. "This is something else!" he said with a wild look in his eye.

Oh, how I wanted to confess everything to him! Warn him of the imminent disaster. Elicit pity for my plight. But there was no time. "Yeah. I gotta get backstage," was all I could manage.

Near-naked big bodies abounded. Upwards of fifty women, those in the show or others helping them get ready, were packed into the dank labyrinth of cinder-block halls and tiny rooms that was "backstage." Each room had huge mirrors with light bulbs like polka dots around the perimeter. Some rooms had tables upon which muscle-bound ladies were perched while their bodies were painted like a canvas: Colette in shades of white and orange with black stripes, Laurie in gold. Others found a few free feet of floor and used the space to paint on their own tan. Even Millie Carter. Hannie Van Aken, the Biker Chic from Holland who looked like the most bodacious female action hero ever conceived of by man, with her butt-long blond hair, huge blue eyes, and abundant bust, sat leaning back in a chair, smoking a cigarette and drinking a Coke. "Millie, darling, what the hell are you doing?" she asked with her gravely Dutch accent. "Don't you think you're dark enough? You're black as the ace of spades!"

Colleene nearly fell off her chair laughing. "Well, look

at me! I'm going to set a national record in drag!" She was super-sporty from the neck down in her sweat suit and sneakers, and all girly from the neck up with model perfect makeup and an upswept hairdo.

Eyeliner, curling irons, and gossip were passed back and forth among the primping women. Dawn was busy getting her blond hair bigger, Robin, her green eyes more prominent, everyone, their skin more tan and glistening. Amazingly the words "I feel fat" seemed to linger in the air ready to descend upon a vulnerable victim who would succumb in a moment of weakness (girlish sideways glances to the mirror checking to see if their tummy stuck out too much betrayed them). Bikini tops had a tough job covering the variations of breasts. Some were all pecs, flat deserts of muscley chests; other breasts were still soft, supple originals; while others looked more like tennis balls placed in flesh-colored socks attached at awkward angles.

The one thing that united everyone in that moment—besides having awesome female muscle—was fear; you could hear it in the nervous hush that occasionally blanketed the rooms and see it in the women's overly animated or slightly stunned expressions. No matter where they came from or what they did, this group was about to perform to a sellout crowd in New York City. No one had any idea how it would turn out, if the crowd would love them or hate them, or if *The Celebration* could even be pulled off at all. They were out of their domain and getting ready to put themselves in the hands of the opinionated public.

I didn't know what to do with myself. I didn't know whether I should go out and sit in the audience. Isn't that what directors did on opening night? Sit there and let people see them watching their own show? Although I wasn't sure I wanted anybody to know who I was. Or should I stay backstage, encouraging the women and telling them they looked great? Dianné had stepped in as the stage manager and was going to "call the show," which meant that she wore a headset to communicate with the lighting and sound guys to let them know when people were ready behind the curtain. Suddenly she came running down the stairs. "Get these ladies lined up!" she yelled. "We're running!"

The Celebration had already begun.

Theater is weird that way. When you're backstage you have no idea what is happening out front, except for when the stage manager says it's your cue. Then the audience watches as you step into a world that has been created by the performers before you. It's kind of like joining a line dance in progress. You hope you step in at just the right time or you can throw everyone off.

I had no idea how the audience was responding or how the women were performing. I wasn't sure I wanted to know. But there was no time for these considerations. I quickly found a locker and shoved my and Dianné's bags into it, figuring I'd change later. I had to find the Ice Queen, Miss America, and the Vampire. None of which proved difficult.

It was Superwoman I couldn't find. Anywhere.

I went upstairs and peeked out with one eye from behind the velvet curtain, praying I'd see the flash of her red cape at the back of the theater, where she was supposed to be. But I didn't.

The heat from the lights was suffocating.

Pacing by the curtain pulls, Dianné hoarsely hissed into her headset, "Where's Superwoman? She's up next! Has anyone seen Superwoman?"

All I wanted was to wear my debut dress.

Bridgett went out with the clan of stagehands to carry the Vampire's fake gravestones offstage. I couldn't persuade any of the crew to feign the accident; being lifted by Superwoman was not their ideal fifteen minutes of fame.

Bridgett volunteered, and she performed her role with panache. She fell, just as planned, under the "weight" of one of the stones. She screamed as if in agony. The Superman theme music blared relentlessly throughout the theater, but Superwoman did not appear.

The stagehands stood in the darkened wings laughing at the poor kid stuck out onstage. Bridgett was doing her best to maintain her distress, but once she stopped screaming, just for a second, to look around for her savior, the styrofoam gravestone shifting easily with her body movement. The audience squirmed in their seats, twisting their heads from side to side, looking for whatever was supposed to happen next.

It smelled like dust, and I could see particles floating in the glare of the lights.

After what felt like five minutes, Superwoman came bounding from the back of the audience, through the crowd, right past the cardboard telephone booth, and heaved herself up onstage like she was climbing out of a pool—pushed herself up to her waist, then dragged one leg up and then the other. (I later learned she had been busy selling her videos in the lobby.) She scooped up Bridgett in one arm, flipping the gravestone weightlessly away from her leg like some incidental car in Godzilla's way. Superwoman struck a biceps pose and then dropped Bridgett off on the edge of the stage so she could squeeze in a lat spread and ab pose before the music ended. The whole time, she battled her cape, which kept swinging around her neck, covering her body.

The crowd didn't seem to care much. As long as female muscle was posing in front of them, they went wild with applause—especially when the pose was the splits and a woman's rear was facing them. Cynthia James as the Vampire was a huge hit, dressed in black stilettos and tattered black rags. She deftly climbed from her coffin and, being one of the more flexible bodybuilders, performed an impressive assortment of cartwheels and splits and hip-grinding maneuvers. The White Lace Affair followed suit, except that Dawn's piece was far more choreographed and the movements coincided with lyrics, for example, she stripped off her jacket and fanned her face when the singer crooned, "It's getting hot in here."

The crowd was less enthusiastic about the emcee segments. They barely clapped following a reading. After White Lace Affair, I slunk out to sit in the audience, just in time to see Cecilia and Montez, our star comediennes, coaxing the seedpod to grow by reading to it from a women's fashion magazine. They were supposed to bring the pod out three times during the show, each time doing something else to make it grow, until it turned into a sunflower at the end. Granted, it was absurd, but that was the point. It was supposed to be so absurd it was funny. It's funny what we do to make ourselves into something other than what we are. But the crowd was not humored. Humorless, in fact. They booed. The actresses hadn't even made it offstage before someone yelled out, "What is this, art?"

I ran into Cecilia backstage. She had tears streaming down her face. "Don't make me go back out there!" she pleaded. Montez looked traumatized as well.

"You were fabulous!" I lied and hugged them both. "The best comediennes ever!"

"They're animals!" Cecilia said and wiped her nose.

"I know. Tough crowd." I hugged them each again and assured them that the worst was over. "Just one more seed-pod scene. And this time it turns into a flower! The crowd will cheer, and they'll finally get it! I promise. You can do it!"

Montez rolled her eyes and walked away, "That's if they don't kill us first."

Lezlie was out front announcing Colleene's lift. Colleene stood in the wings with her fancy hair, wearing short red weightlifting overalls, rolling her shoulders, and shaking out her legs to get ready to set a record. Artie Drescheler, the head of the National Weightlifting Association's board of directors, was sitting in the audience to officially witness the event. He had supplied the weights and the special weightlifting bar that would be used. He had also tested the stage floor to make sure that when Colleene dropped the 231 pounds of iron, it did not go crashing through to the basement.

Lezlie quieted the crowd. Colleene walked up to the weights blowing through pursed lips. She bent from the waist with her knees slightly loose, wrapped her hands around the bar, and secured her grip. With a quick whip and guttural growl she lifted it to just below her chin, held it there for a breath or two, and, howling, shot that bar straight up above her head. She staggered to the side a few steps under the weight, but finally secured a stance and stood victorious before the roaring crowd. Then she let the hefty mass drop to the floor and did a goofy triumphant jig. It was a sight to behold: the joy of achievement and the beauty of something actually going right in the show.

Next up was a special tribute. Laurie had had a bronze statue made to present to the all-around unstoppable athlete and female bodybuilding's limit pusher, Bev Francis.

In her introduction, Laurie listed just a few of Bev's accomplishments, which include an Australian shot-put record from her early days on the Australian national track and field team, five years as the undefeated world powerlifting champion (she left forty world records for her successors to beat when she retired in 1985), and numerous bodybuilding titles, including first place in the IFBB World Championship. Bev had since retired from competing and at the time of the show was running the Bev Francis Gold's Gym on Long Island. When Bev stepped out onstage in a tasteful pantsuit to accept her award, she received a standing ovation. It went on. And on. And on. And on.

It's too bad that the final seedpod sequence had to come next. Or maybe the crowd was feeling inspired and therefore forgiving. In the previous episodes, Montez and Cecilia had carried a big stuffed seed out onstage. In this final act, however, the seed was a real person (a college friend to whom I am indebted for life) dressed up in a felt sunflower costume. Montez and Cecilia did their duty and sprinkled NutraGro on the reluctant pod and were just about to give up hope that the seed would ever blossom. And then, before the impatient audience, a leaf shot up from the sunflower, and then another leaf, and a skinny stalk began to grow until the sunflower stretched up toward the sky. Perfectly in character, Montez and Cecilia celebrated their bloom, and the crowd joined in, everyone relieved that the torture was finally over.

Through all of this I had been watching from the wings, but I sneaked out front to see the next performance. I found an empty seat on the perimeter of the theater, folded my arms across my chest, and waited. It was time for Magna Mater.

The curtain opened on the chorus of actresses standing in two perfect rows, dressed in long black gowns, like fancy judges but without the wigs. They moved in unison toward the front of the stage and stopped right where they were supposed to. So far so good. Laurie crouched next to the faux mountain, looking like one herself. There was silence. She raised her head slightly, shooting a look to the chorus for her cue. They looked back to her for theirs. Laurie had forgotten that it was her movement that was supposed to start everything. Neither would begin without a sign from the other. The audience waited for something to happen.

I stopped breathing altogether.

Finally, Cecilia's voice broke the silence:

"How could it be?
That they could treat me so
I, the mind of the past,
To be driven under the ground, outcast, like dirt!
Earth, ah, earth, what is this agony that crawls
under my ribs?
Night, hear me, oh night, mother
They have wiped me out and with hard hands and
treachery have taken my old rights away."

Laurie slowly stood up and made mild gestures with her arms, but her shoulders hung low and her head sagged. She looked down to find the steps behind the rock to help her rise. Then, the chorus kicked in with a second verse, which seemed to propel her.

"From the darkness of her glance
Glares an angry dragon's eye
See her thousand oars advance!
See ten thousand arrows fly!
The mighty chariot rides before;
Columns of warriors in their pride,
Like a vast flood leap and roar,
As none can stem that ocean-tide."

Laurie spread her arms out to each side and curled her fists up, pulling them in toward her shoulders for a double-biceps pose. A faint smile sped past her lips as she twisted her torso to each wing of the audience. She posed her way up and over the mountain, failing to take her time at the top to display her infamous lat spread, as we had planned. Instead, as if she didn't want to be seen, she hurried through poses she made up as she went, getting to the other side long before the chorus launched into its final verse:

"I have been in many shapes.
I have been a shining star.
I have been a word in a book.
I have been the book itself.
I have been a director in a battle.
There is nothing which I have not been.
I have been a tree in a covert
With the wind and rain howling through my bow
Putting forth new leaves
Changing form and being renewed."

Laurie stood awkwardly at the bottom of the rock, striking fleeting poses. When the chorus was quiet, she took a bow, forced a smile, and walked off.

It was sad seeing Laurie look like the wisp of the woman I had originally met and awful watching the drawn-out fizzle of her performance. It was more than I could bear.

I slunk backstage. All I wanted was to wear my dress. Logic at that time told me that putting it on could salvage my debut. I knew that was ridiculous, but I couldn't help myself. I wore a face that told everyone I was extremely busy. I was the playwright and director after all. I could have had something important to do, such as looking for the next performer or finding Cleopatra's crown. No one would ever dream that I was actually escaping into the labyrinth to get dressed up.

It was cool and dank, like a basement in the middle of spring rains. Dirty lightbulbs emitted gray light that dingily and sporadically lit up the cement floor. I knew the lockers lined the walls of one of the halls, but which one I wasn't quite sure. I hadn't paid attention when I shoved my things in earlier. I clumsily tripped more deeply into the labyrinth, until I finally came to a row of dirty butter-colored lockers defaced with gouges and dents. This was it. I slipped my finger through the cold, metal grip and pulled up and out, but the door wouldn't budge. There was no combination built in, just a handle with a little hole for a lock to slide through. I yanked at it again. No give.

I stood transfixed by the stuckness of the locker, looking from side to side, willing someone to appear. I tried again, putting my left foot up against the neighboring locker and pulled with everything I had. Nothing. I began to cry. I would have nothing to wear for the Finale. I hit the locker with the flat of my hand and inflicted dents with the rubber toe of my shoe, yelling, "Open! Damn it! Open!"

I don't know how long I was there before a janitor appeared with a crow bar to open the locker. He arrived just as a voice echoed through the halls, "Kristin, where are you? You're on! It's the Finale! She's calling your name!" I threw on my dress and left my things lying on the floor. I ran up the stairs to the wings of the theater, where I stood watching Laurie, who seemed to have recovered command of herself, standing centerstage, wearing a strapless maroon-velvet dress. She held one arm up to block the glare of the lights and held a microphone with the other, calling, "Kristin, where are you? Will someone get Kristin?" She was strutting back and forth across the stage, stopping periodically to hug one of the participants.

"Dianné! Where is Dianné?" she called out.

A pack of female African American drummers stood in a cluster, stage right, pounding out a steady beat. All the women milled about in full costume, dancing a little, and stopping to pose for the crowd, each one giving the audience one last look at her physique. Tigress Colette next to Superwoman Nicole next to Cleopatra Linda next to Shaman Robin next to White Lace Dawn and right on down the line, more than twenty towers of female muscle, dressed up and showing it all off. In the center of the menagerie, Cecilia, Montez, Lezlie, Rochelle, Cindy, Bridgett, and Starr, all dressed in red skirts and tops that they had scrounged together somehow, were dancing their hearts out. They were the only ones who stuck with the choreographed ending, and while dancing might not have been their forte, they hit every move.

I stood watching from behind the curtain. I didn't want to go onstage, but Laurie kept calling for me, so I stepped out and hid behind the Ice Queen.

"C'mon everybody!" Laurie waved her arms, rousing the audience to cheers. She turned and whispered something to Doughdee, who then grabbed Colleene, who in turn organized a few women to scoop Laurie up from behind and hoist her high in the air. Laurie feigned surprise, mouthing the words, "What are they doing?" Once steady in her position on their shoulders, Laurie raised her fists and hit a double-biceps pose while the rest of us clapped our hands in time with the drumbeat, shuffled our feet from side to side, smiled and looked from each other to Laurie to the audience and back again as if trying to find somebody who looked like they knew what, exactly, it was we were celebrating.

17

After *The Celebration*

I n the theater world, the party following the close of a show is usually a raucous affair. The stress of weeks of rehearsal, stage fright, and general tension blows off in hours of dancing and singing and replaying odd events from the run of the show. Arms are wrapped around others' shoulders and old show tunes are sung with bellowing voices. It is a time when hatchets are buried and animosity is laid to rest.

I was looking forward to *The Celebration*'s after party. I

wanted to cut loose. I wanted to hug the bodybuilders and have the bodybuilders hug me. I wanted to laugh with the actresses and recall, now that the horror was over, how Cindy had forgotten her lines when she was introducing Cleopatra. I wanted the laugh to become hilarious, with the need to gasp for breath. And then I wanted the laugh to turn to sighs as we agreed that none of it mattered anyway, because Cleopatra's entrance was so spectacular with trumpeting horns and beefy men that the image of Linda Wood-Hoyte being delivered to the stage on a gold litter would be forever etched in people's memories. I wanted my laugh with Laurie to be mixed with tears to wash away the ill will. I wanted to recount how we first met and together confirm, once and for all, that it really was Fate that drew us together; perhaps for reasons we didn't quite understand, but we'd eye each other knowingly, secretly trusting that it would be revealed with time.

When I arrived at the party, I expected to hear cheers and music and to see people dancing. It was strangely quiet, however. I waited my turn at the buffet, filled my plate, and took a seat at a round, clothed table, figuring the party would surely get going soon. Rochelle and Cecilia sat beside me, and we began to make small talk, asking questions about each other's lives, as if we had just met for the first time. Lezlie and Montez joined us, and we were just about to enjoy a collective sigh of relief when a man sat next to me and introduced himself.

"Are you a bodybuilder?" he asked.

"Um, no. I'm not a bodybuilder." I didn't look like a bodybuilder.

"Are you with the show?" he asked.

"Yeah, I was the director of the show." Finally someone was interested in who I was.

"Wow," he said, his eyes wandering to other tables. The conversation ended there, and I let my eyes follow his. At each of the surrounding tables, a bodybuilder was entertaining a circle of fans. Miss America Karla Nelson stood a head taller than most of her adorers, who lavished her with praise and booked sessions with her. Doughdee Marie was signing autographs. She wore a low-, low-cut shirt and used her biceps to plump up her breasts as she held programs in front of her, scribbling messages onto them. That's when it became clear. This was no after party. This was the V.I.P. party. This was the special bonus for the men who had paid $125 a ticket. This was the party for the celebrated tribe of which I was not a part.

I suddenly felt very lonely. Even though the devotion that was being doled out in bucketfuls to the bodybuilders was not exactly the type of attention I wanted, after the weeks of insanity, not being noticed at all was more than I could bear.

I decided to leave. I hugged the actresses one by one. We swore we'd have a reunion, and I made my way through the crowd of "V.I.P.s" to the exit.

On my way out, I saw Laurie. She had an aftershow glow.

It is always awkward to be the friend of an artist when his or her opening or show hasn't gone so well. I never know what to say. Do you pretend and say, "Great show?" Or do you acknowledge the failure and offer an encouraging hug? It is even more awkward when you are at a show put on by an artistic team, and one of the artists is you and the other artist thinks everything went swimmingly. I didn't know what to say to Laurie. We suffered a self-conscious silence, and then I said, "Congratulations. Thanks for everything." And she said, "Great job." We hugged, and I was on my way.

Grand Central Station was just a few blocks away. It was late, but I walked. I was no longer scared of the city. In the months that I had been preparing for the show, I'd come to think of it less like a jungle full of man-eating animals and more like a complex ecosystem that you had to respect, but that wasn't necessarily going to harm you; kind of like nature, only different. I'd learned that New York's "elements" were car exhaust and rivers of people and the deafening din of jackhammers and freewheeling cabbies who constantly reinterpret traffic signals. I'd been cornered on the subway by a woman who started pelting me with uncooked macaroni noodles and insisted that she knew me, that I'd made her coffee once, and threatened she wouldn't let me off the train until I admitted that I was Russian (which I am not); I tried to remain calm while the rest of the passengers looked on, and at the next stop I simply got off, stood safely on the platform, and watched the subway whisk macaroni lady away. I had survived.

On that night in November, I would actually have welcomed an encounter with a crazy person. It would have made more sense than what I had just gone through. It would have been even better if the crazy person had crossed my path, like sometimes happens in the movies, and said something random that somehow made everything make sense, like "I know the king was naked!"

No such luck.

I stood at the heart of Grand Central terminal waiting

for my train next to the circular info booth with the glowing clock that looms above it like a helium balloon. It's the best place to stand to avoid getting bumped by the commuters; either there or against the towering slabs of marble that are the walls. There seems to be an invisible line around the booth that people rushing to catch their connection don't cross. Most are making a beeline either to or from the trains and having to actually go around something adds to their travel time by at least five seconds so they avoid the problem entirely by keeping their distance from the information booth. So, you can stand in the middle of Grand Central fairly safe from the whirl around you. I looked up at the ceiling to kill time.

It needed a cleaning. Years of the city's hot air had risen, collecting every blackened particle of exhaust produced by the vents and tailpipes and mouths of the churning metropolis, and deposited itself on the celestial ceiling soaring some one hundred feet above the bustling hub. One could faintly see the grand plan of the stars struggling to depict constellations like Orion, Pegasus, and Cancer. The images drawn from the sea of starry possibilities were insistent through the sooty cloak of time. Hovering over the wild thrust of Manhattan, their presence seemed somehow ridiculous in their implication, as if they were calling out, "Look up! Here lies perfect order!" It was almost laughable.

Who first saw a hunter in that particular arrangement of stars anyway? Why a hunter and not a boat? Why a crab and not a butterfly? Why not a scroll or a shoe or a chair? And how is it that those ancient blueprints have persisted through the ages? Their connect-the-dots outlines seemed more like ghosts of order defined by and for a different age, reminding us that humans have been trying to understand the ways of the world since the beginning of time.

"You know the sky is backwards."

I looked around to see who was talking and noticed that the Metropolitan Transportation Authority worker in the information booth had switched on his microphone and was addressing me.

"The sky on the ceiling. It's backwards," he broadcasted.

"I'm sorry?" I walked closer to the booth, because I wasn't sure I was hearing him correctly.

"The French guy who painted it back in the early nineteen hundreds got the perspective all wrong. It's supposed to be a Mediterranean night sky, but he painted it backwards, so those constellations up there are all screwed up."

"A Mediterranean night sky over Manhattan?" It didn't make sense.

"Either that or somewhere in Texas. It's supposed to be at thirty-five degrees latitude, so I guess it could be anywhere along there, really."

"No kidding?" I asked.

"Go figure," he said.

I took my place among the sea of bobbing heads and shuffled toward the underground corridor to meet my train home feeling unsettled by the notion that the stories we tell ourselves and others are often only partly true.

Epilogue

How do you judge the success of a show? Well, there are the obvious ways—it can have a long run. It can be sold out. It can receive standing ovations night after night. Critics can love it, though critics can hate it and still some might argue that a show is a critical success. Aspects of the show can shine—the score, the script, the acting—and save it from complete doom. And sometimes, beauty is in the eye of the beholder. Sometimes, it's just a personal thing—a show just hits the spot for a certain person on a certain day. And so it was with *The Celebration*.

For me, it was an event in my life that I couldn't even talk about for many years. When it was over, I knew I wouldn't be getting a call from the Broadway producer to work on a show she was producing. I knew my ex-professor wouldn't be lavishing praise on me in the *Village Voice*. The fact that it was sold out—knowing how many people actually witnessed the event—only added insult to injury. My self-confidence was shaken, and it would be years before I ventured into my own creative project again. Hiding under a blanket for the next twenty years was about all I could see myself doing.

Others, however, had a completely different experience of *The Celebration*.

Colette Guimond: "I thought the show was great. I loved the whole idea behind it, that women can be muscular, but still feminine and sexy in their own way. Just because a woman has muscles does not mean she has to look like a man. I wish Laurie would do more of them, and maybe it could become a world production, like the Cirque du Soleil."

Bill Wick: "She did pull it off, but it didn't change the world. The people who showed up are the people who get off on female muscle. They were so excited because they got to wrestle women like Karla Nelson. They'd say, 'Oh my god, I got to wrestle Karla Nelson! Isn't that great! I even got to talk to her and she gave me her autograph.' I'd ask, 'How'd you do?' and they'd say, 'What do mean how'd I do?' and I'd say, 'Well, did you win?' They didn't even try to win."

Dawn Whitham: "The show was awesome. I loved the fact that Laurie was promoting female bodybuilders in an artistic light. You don't just have to see them on the stage flexing in a posing suit with veins popping out of their head. I just wish that there were people like her who continued the forward motion. It seems to me that if anyone would promote it, it would take off."

John Nafpliotis: "It was one of the first times that you saw women who didn't diet or try to outperform one another. It was a breath of fresh air without the judging process. You could really appreciate the fact that none of them were being graded. It would have been nice if Laurie's vision seeped into the bodybuilding world, but as the sport is set up, it won't accommodate a range of physiques and conditioning."

Robin Parker: "It was a way to be creative and not have the traditional constraints, limitations, and demands that are made on you in regular bodybuilding. I thought it was fantastic and a great opportunity. Her whole idea about this being a major feminist thing turned a lot of people off, though. She couldn't keep her politics out of it. So we were like, 'Okay, we'll take what we can get, I guess.' But people were just happy to be there. It was so much fun. I don't think the show had any impact on the IFBB whatsoever. Not that I could tell."

Dan Denton (in *MuscleMag International*): "I've got to give Laurie Fierstein a lot of credit. Actually, the entire world of bodybuilding should give Laurie a whole world of credit, because she did something for the awareness of muscle that may have propelled it ahead by fifty years. It wasn't such a hard task after all, and I'm shocked that nobody has had the nerve, or guts, to do it before. She did what many muscle people fear to do—communicate with the 'mainstream media.'"

Linda Wood-Hoyte: "It was a crowning moment for the sport of bodybuilding and for me personally. It was one of the most fun things I had done in the sport. The sky was the limit as far as creativity was concerned. You could use your creativity to the fullest and I did. You can't get any better than that. Laurie did an excellent job. As far as the sport was concerned, however, it wasn't a sanctioned event, but I think the bodybuilding community received it extremely well. I'm not sure if the general public really understood it though."

Charles Peeples (in *MuscleMag International*): "This is the showcase that muscular women have needed for so long, away from the competition, with its politically charged landscape and questionable purpose. Here women do not vie to be judged better than one another, but are free to *create*, to express their whole persona without the arbitrary constraints which have made competitive bodybuilding a crapshoot . . . Perhaps it's not for everyone, but the absence of the ogre crowd from the audience will scarcely hurt things. Here is the road to the sky—perhaps, as I wrote once before, the Met or La Scala. Not a contest, but a Happening.

To Laurie, to the women who performed, to the people behind the scenes, to those who came to look, to all who believed, drive on! Broadway's half a block away, and by George, I think we've got it!"

Laurie Fierstein was not available for comment.